MADHYA PRADESH GROWTH STORY

MADHYA PRADESH GROWTH STORY

UNFOLDING AN INNOVATIVE BUSINESS MODEL FOR GROWTH

PRATAP VERMA

MANJUL
Manjul Publishing House

First published in India by

Manjul Publishing House
Corporate and Editorial Office
• 2nd Floor, Usha Preet Complex, 42 Malviya Nagar, Bhopal 462 003 - India
Sales and Marketing Office
• 7/32, Ground Floor, Ansari Road, Daryaganj, New Delhi 110 002 - India
Website: www.manjulindia.com
Distribution Centres
Ahmedabad, Bengaluru, Bhopal, Kolkata, Chennai,
Hyderabad, Mumbai, New Delhi, Pune

Madhya Pradesh Growth Story: Unfolding An Innovative Business Model for Growth by *Pratap Verma*

This edition first published in 2016

ISBN 978-81-8322-720-9

Printed and bound in India by Replika Press Pvt. Ltd.

This book has been prepared to provide an informative source of details about the state of Madhya Pradesh and its economic growth. Whereas every effort has been made to ensure correct and accurate information, the author and the publisher wish to clarify that they are absolved from legal liability should any discrepancies be found.

This book is dedicated to the people of
Madhya Pradesh

CONTENTS

PREFACE

The purpose of this book is to enlighten governments, organisations and business leaders as to how to lead in a fast changing world where volatility, ambiguity, uncertainty and complexity are the new challenges for governance, leadership and management. The Indian state of Madhya Pradesh has just shown that by its phenomenal growth in last ten years.

Madhya Pradesh, the second largest Indian state with a population of 72 million has registered a compounded annual GDP growth rate of 10% consistently since the year 2011. The growth in the agriculture GDP is even higher at 20% since the year 2011 and is the highest in the world. This book narrates the story of 'why and how' this growth has taken place. According to the latest figures, the unemployment rate in Madhya Pradesh is at all time low @ 2.9% as against India's average of 4.9%.

This is the story of the stupendous growth Madhya Pradesh has achieved whose seeds were implanted by conceptualising the State Global Investors' Summit in the year 2005. This is the story of the commitment and political will of its Chief Minister Shivraj Singh Chauhan who led from the front with credibility and honest intentions that gave him mass support. The emotional connectivity became the success mantra.

The success story of Madhya Pradesh has been achieved through a gaming model wherein political leaders, bureaucrats, investors and other relevant stakeholders join together through crowd sourcing platforms ,such as State Global Investors' Summits, community gatherings [*Panchayats*] and think tanks [*Manthan*], etc. The fusion of these platforms acted as catalysts and prime mover for Madhya Pradesh government to become seamless and borderless. This new gaming model fostered creativity and series of innovations in the State Government's working.

The State Government has been able to create a single window online system for investments and service guarantee schemes. These initiatives are helping the government to digitise itself for efficient and effective governance.

It is making the Madhya Pradesh government more service oriented and participatory in approach. The tendency of administering by command, regulation and control is now being used judiciously. The net result is that there is efficiency and effectiveness at the same time due to synchronicity of purpose among diverse sections of people.

This new gaming model could be an eye-opener and a game changer for governments and organisations around the world.

This is a hands-on story since I was a member of the pioneering team that conceptualised and implemented the gaming model of State Global Investors' Summits.

Indeed it was my pleasure and privilege to work with brilliant and committed officers like Rakesh Sahni, Avani

Vaish, Satya Prakash, Raghav Chandra, Iqbal Singh Bains, Manoj Shrivastava, Praveen Garg and S K Mishra during my journey with State Global Investors' Summits as an Industrial Promotion Advisor to Madhya Pradesh Trade and Investment Facilitation Corporation [TRIFAC]

Pratap Verma
email: pratap.verma@gmail.com.
www.facebook.com/pratap.verma.146

1

THE NEW DAWN IN MADHYA PRADESH

This book is inspired by what the Indian Prime Minister Narendra Modi spoke about Madhya Pradesh at the State's Global Investors' Summit on October 9, 2014 at Indore. This is what Narendra Modi said on that day, 'I am sure Madhya Pradesh will be a driving force in India's economy. This state can cater to the entire nation. The world must know that a state has been growing steadily in the last few years. Even God must talk about Madhya Pradesh.'

Well, I am not God but certainly I can talk and write about Madhya Pradesh because the seeds of phenomenal growth of Madhya Pradesh lie in its innovative initiative of Global Investor Summit conceptualised in the year 2005/2006. I was fortunate to be a member of the pioneering team that sowed the seeds of growth of Madhya Pradesh led amicably by Shivraj Singh Chauhan, the most innovative Chief Minister the state ever had. This I can say with confidence since I had personally known most of the state chief ministers beginning from Pandit Ravishankar Shukul [Nov, 1956] the first chief minister of new Madhya Pradesh.

Presented here is the untold story of growth of Madhya Pradesh with critical analysis of leadership, governance and management. It's a story of how Madhya Pradesh evolved as well as grew as a developed state. It's a story of connectivity and emotions that leveraged the usual system-based progress. It's a unique balance of efficiency and effectiveness as also that of the mind and the heart. Shivraj Singh has often said that 'I do not speak from the mind, I speak from the heart. Invest in Madhya Pradesh. It is not only developing itself on all parameters, but also guiding the nation's overall development, your effort will not go as waste.'

He spoke from the heart but implemented with will, commitment, strategies and right use of resources through shrewd application of mind and the collective mind set generated by emotional connectivity.

He is a mass leader who is able to connect with most people because of humility, sense of purpose and honest and credible intentions.

This is what the leading industrial icons of India have said about Madhya Pradesh:

I am very much impressed to see the growth environment in the state under the leadership of dynamic Chief Minister. India is on the resurgent path of growth and Madhya Pradesh is already on the way. This 11% growth is just a beginning. Madhya Pradesh has the potential to do much more than this. I can say Madhya Pradesh would be the digital capital of India and I say Madhya Pradesh Mera [my] Pradesh [state].

Mukesh Ambani, Chairman, Managing Director,
Reliance Industries Limited

Gujarat and Madhya Pradesh states are the two best Indian States for future investments.

Kumar Manglam Birla,
Aditya Birla Group

Madhya Pradesh is well positioned as an investment destination globally and strategies are already set for further development. We have India's only automatic leather manufacturing unit at Dewas, now TCS is expanding its activities in a new integrated campus at Indore which will provide employment to 10,000 IT professionals.

Cyrus Mistry, Chairman,
Tata Sons Ltd.

This is my fourth Global Investor's Summit in Madhya Pradesh and I have seen one of the greatest transformations in India by this state. This is because of the visionary leadership of the Chief Minister; he is the champion of the champions.

Anil Ambani, CEO
Reliance Group ADA

I am impressed with the kind of leadership provided by Chief Minister of Madhya Pradesh, the state has made unbelievable growth in the Gross State Domestic Product, per capita income, Agricultural production and Irrigation, and Power generation.

Gautam Adani, Chairman,
Adani Group

The state has all the resources and potential earlier but it was only leadership, which has made Madhya Pradesh as the fastest developing state in the country. As the country is lucky to have a Prime Minister like Shri Narendra Modi, the state is lucky to have a Chief Minister like Shri Shivraj Singh Chauhan. Madhya Pradesh ITC story of village and agricultural development is a case study taught in Harvard Business School, from cotton to fashion, cattle to dairy and from farm to fork there is a lot of potential in the field of value addition in the agriculture sector.

Y C Deveshwar, Chairman,
ITC

Madhya Pradesh is one of the fastest growing states of the country. With such a vision, Madhya Pradesh very soon will shine on the top.

A M Naik,
Larsen and Toubro

We have completed 27 successful years in Madhya Pradesh. When I asked my officers to give me the points to be raised before the Honourable Chief Minister during the meeting, the reply was we already got everything we want and there is nothing to discuss, this illustrates the working style of Madhya Pradesh.

Adi Godrej, Chairman,
Godrej Group

We are impressed with the transparent policies and support provided by Madhya Pradesh Government. The local man-power is fantastic. This is our biggest tractor manufacturing facility in India and we are exporting tractors to 70 countries. Ek naya itihaas likhne John Deere Madhya Pradesh ke saath hai [John Deere is with Madhya Pradesh in scripting its new development story].

John Stone, Global Director,
John Deere

We are already in power sector and I can say Madhya Pradesh is a place where you can plan the investment and implement it.

Shashi Ruia, Chairman,
Essar Group

Growth and leadership are amazing in this state.

Kishore Biyani, CEO,
Future Group

Today Madhya Pradesh is a power surplus state with an installed capacity of 15,500 megawatt, 62,000 kilometres of rebuilt state roads [inclusive of multi-lane, state, district, and village roads]. Its irrigation facilities stand at 3.6 million hectares. Shivraj Singh's leadership has been able to lift the state out of the *Bimarou* [acronym for undeveloped states: Bihar, Madhya Pradesh, Rajasthan, Odisha and Uttar Pradesh] tag.

Compare the above with the state of affairs when the BJP came to power in December 2003, the installed power was 4,800 megawatt, there was not one single good road in the state; even the distance between Bhopal and Indore about 200 kilometres was covered in 6 hours [now 3 hours] and irrigation facilities were available only in an area of 0.75 million hectares.

The development of infrastructure has enabled the people to help themselves. The enabled environment is clearly visible by the GSDP [Gross State Domestic product] figures showing CAGR [compounded annual growth rate] of more than 10% per annum for last 3 years; being one of the highest in the country at 11.08% in 2014–2015 [it was less than 4% between the years 1998–2003]. This is remarkable considering the global economic slowdown because of dot.com bubble and steep fall of growth in the year 2007 the world over. The GSDP growth in agriculture has been the highest in the world for last few years. The average GSDP growth since the year 2011 to 2015 [four years] is above 20%.

Indeed it is some kind of miracle but how did it happen? The credit naturally has to be bestowed on the head of the state – the Chief Minister Shivraj Singh but the question arises that as to how he performed such a feat. He had a humble background – to achieve this kind of miraculous feat, he required a solid support of a knowledgeable team that could help him in meeting his vision and dreams. By nature he is very affable and humble, empathises very well with people. Also he is very good at learning, adopting and adapting new things. These attributes enable him to connect with people emotionally that enables the delivery at the ground level. This gives him credibility along with an unflinching trust of the people. The emotional connectivity leads to synchronicity with the masses.

The secret of his success lies in the socio-economic business model created by a series of Global Investors' Summits process that started in January 2007 at the Khajuraho Investors' meet followed by road shows at Mumbai, New Delhi and Bengaluru. After that the first Global Investor's Summit was held at Indore in October 2007. Since then regular global investors' summits have taken place in 2010, 2012 and 2014, now the next global investors' meet is scheduled in October 2016 at Indore. These investors' summits paved the way for growth awareness in the state, which also helped the Chief Minister to realise and conceptualise the bigger state picture. Investors' summits provided the tool to strategise the growth parameters needed for a state like Madhya Pradesh. It enabled Madhya Pradesh to leverage its strengths and potential. Madhya Pradesh's slow growth was attributed to its geographical configuration of being a land locked state but now the weakness has become its logistic strength.

Madhya Pradesh now has an ideal ratio of GSDP components of economy, Primary sector [30%], Tertiary sector [25%] and Services sector [45%] commensurate with present state of Indian economy that would further lead it to the arena of a knowledge-based society.

The above ratio provides a balance between all sectors with inclusive growth which is amply reflected by rate of unemployment in the state of Madhya Pradesh that is lower than most of the other states.

The Agro Business model of agriculture, making agriculture a profitable business model has paid off and has given rich dividends to farmers. At more than 20% CAGR growth in last 4 years the Agriculture GDP rise in Madhya Pradesh is the highest in the world. It's pertinent to ask as to where do the ideas for this exponential growth come from; once again the answer is Global Investor's Summits.

The ensuing story shall reveal the power of Global Investor's Summits. The investor's summits have flowered into an exponential growth engine for the state of Madhya Pradesh. This has been possible due to the political will and commitment, bureaucratic cooperation and participation of investors and other stakeholders like the Tiger project, the Investor's summit provided the backward integration of all connected processes.

The Investors' Summit were not merely the instrument for attracting investments [as is the general perception] but a tool for Governance, growth and galvanising of politics [all parties], bureaucracy and investors and other connected stakeholders. All worked together towards a common vision and goals of making Madhya Pradesh a progressive state. Global Investors' summit changed the mind sets of people and had been a game changer like it has been in Gujarat.

In the next few chapters we shall take you to the fascinating journey of the 'Global Investors' Summit' concept and reveal for the first time, how it changed Madhya Pradesh and similarly as to how it can change other states of India and elsewhere in the world.

It's a story of working together and unleashing the power of Alchemy of 'I, You, We and Us.'

This is how CMIE [Centre for Monitoring Indian Economy] has reported about Madhya Pradesh – Excerpts.

Madhya Pradesh had the highest growth in GSDP in 2013–2014 – Growth led mainly by agriculture sector

'Madhya Pradesh outpaced all the major states to show the highest growth in Gross State Domestic Product [GSDP] in 2013–2014. The state's GSDP registered a double-digit growth of 11.1% at constant prices, up from 9.9% in 2012–2013. Its GSDP thus stood at ₹2,38,500 crores [US$37 billion] in 2013–2014 at constant prices.

'Madhya Pradesh has been showing a strong growth of above 9% since 2009–2010. Also, most of this growth in the recent years is propelled by a high growth in the agriculture and allied sector supplemented by a modest growth in the services sector. Growth rates in these two sectors have helped tide over the sluggish industrial performance in the state. Moreover, the per capita NDP [Net Domestic Product] in the state has also been growing at a sturdy pace of around 8% since 2008. It grew by 9.6% in 2012–2013.

'The share of agriculture with its allied sectors in GSDP was 29% while that of industry and services sector was 25.6% and 45.4%, respectively in 2013–2014. The agriculture and allied sector share has been rising since 2008–2009, while that of the industrial sector has been declining. This is in contrast to all the major states, which are seeing a decline in the agriculture and allied sector share in their GSDP.

'Much of the growth in this year too can be accorded to the agriculture and its allied sectors. It manifested a growth of 23.3%, over an 18.6% rise in 2012–2013. Within the sector, agriculture alone recorded a growth of 25%. It has been seeing a remarkable growth of around 20% since the last three years. It had fourth highest share of 8% in India's agriculture sector GDP in 2012–2013. Further, the state ranks second highest in food grain production in the country, only after Uttar Pradesh. The state is also known for its non-cereal crops, especially oilseeds.

'The growth in agriculture can be attributed to the additional irrigation facilities created in the state in the last three years.'

The GDP of Madhya Pradesh in 2014–2015 has been ₹5,08,006 crores [US$ 85 billion] at current prices and ₹2,53,530 crores [US$ 40 billion] at constant prices.

Therefore the readers would observe that Global Investors' Summits are not only for garnering the investments but they have also set out clear direction – a road map for future growth, by clearly spelling out potential and opportunities in the state. Finally they bring government and investors together for carving win-win situations. The introduction of the Single-window concept has made the administration seamless and borderless and that speeds up the process of economic growth.

Shivraj Singh continuously reinvented the Global Investors' Summit model by enhancing its power after initiating the first such event in 2007. In the 2014 Global Investors' Summit, 28 countries participated and 8 countries were partners to the event. The prime minster Modi was the chief guest for the event – he complimented the Madhya Pradesh Government for using the Global Investors' Summit as an economic innovation tool. The Global Investors' Summit is a gaming model that joins government, relevant stake holders such as industrialists, bankers, investors, education and health sectors etc. by crowd sourcing them at one place, wherein everyone gets a chance to speak up their mind and heart in an open manner and carve out their own roles for meeting shared vision and goals. The government adopts a facilitating environment and is an empathetic listener. It asks for stake holders' inputs on ways and means to attract investment by creating an enabling environment through right kind of policies, political will, vision, goals and incentives. Shivraj Singh has intuitively extended and used this gaming model in other domains as well such as social engineering. The success of community gatherings [*Panchayats*] of various sections of the society, the water management of irrigation fields through convergence of technologies [especially mobile phones] and holding of *Manthan* [a kind of thinking conclave] have changed the socio-economic scenario of the state with accelerated speed, the transition in the economy has been rapid as the results are there for everyone to experience – see for themselves. The seamlessness of government administration is quite evident from the functioning of Trade and Investment Facilitation Corporation [TRIFAC] that acts as a single-window for investments in the state and virtually works like a Chief Minister's secretariat.

As compared to the investment received in tertiary sector in the period 1998–2003 of ₹640 Crores, the state has garnered on the ground an investment of ₹61,000 Crores [US$9.1 billion] between the years 2004–2015.

The GSDP growth in secondary [Manufacturing sector] sector is slated to grow at an accelerated pace since projects worth ₹20,000 crores [US$3 billion] are in advanced stage of completion. Therefore it is very likely that the GSDP [Gross State Domestic Product] of Madhya Pradesh will be above 10% over the next five years.

We shall see as we go through the story as to how the seeds sown by the presentations at global investors' summits fuelled growth of Madhya Pradesh and has made it the number one state in Agriculture. Industrialisation had been possible through growth of infrastructure mainly power, roads and water management. We shall discuss as to how it has made bureaucracy people friendly.

2

HOW THE STORY OF GLOBAL INVESTORS' SUMMIT BUSINESS MODEL EVOLVED

On 24th December, 2003, Ms Uma Bharti was installed as the chief minister of Madhya Pradesh. She spearheaded the BJP's election campaign on the plank of *Sadak* [road], *Bijli* [electrical power] and water. Ms Bharti won hands down with absolute majority. At this point of time the economy as stated in the earlier chapter was in doldrums.

She was a chief minister in a hurry and was very keen in rebuilding the economy of the state. Several key positions were immediately filled with dynamic officers who had proven delivery track records. One such department was Commerce and Industry. Within a fortnight of her assuming office, she appointed Vishwapati Trivedi [1977 Batch IAS Officer] as Principal Secretary and Raghav Chandra [1982 IAS batch – a Harvard alumnus] as Managing Director Madhya Pradesh Industrial Development Corporation

[MPSIDC] and Madhya Pradesh Road Corporation. Commerce and Industry Minister Kailash Chawla, able and experienced with an impeccable track record was told to speed up the process of Industrialisation. Since continuous 24 x 7 power supply is the basic requirement of progress, another very dynamic officer Rakesh Sahni [1971 batch, IAS] was made the Principal Secretary Power. Uma Bharti met the local industrialists. After an extensive dialogue with local Industry associations – she also had an opportunity to address the Federation of Indian Chamber of Commerce and Industry [FICCI] in January, 2004 in New Delhi at its AGM function. As per the feedback she received from prominent Indian Industrialists, she told the Commerce and Industry Department to carve out a new Industrial Policy for Madhya Pradesh, which was more attractive than other states to woo the investors.

Thus the trio of Kailash Chawla, Vishwapati Trivedi, and Raghav Chandra were told to interact within the state, nationally and globally to make an attractive industrial promotion policy. The Chief Minister had given clear instructions to make the new policy applicable from the new fiscal year, i.e. 1st April, 2004.

The team began the exercise earnestly. That time, I happened to be the Secretary of Federation of Madhya Pradesh Chamber of Commerce and Industry [FMPCCI], which is the apex body of Industry Associations and Trade in Madhya Pradesh. I was very actively consulted in framing of the policy. FMPCCI also provided the platform for interacting with other entrepreneurs and industrialists. Here it will be prudent to give some of my background, I studied mechanical engineering from Maulana Azad National Institute of Technology Bhopal in 1969 [It was then MACT] and till 1999 I had worked in industry with long term associations with three leading companies out of the top 100 Fortune global companies before taking over as Secretary – FMPCCI [Federation of Madhya Pradesh Chamber of Commerce and Industry]; since my father was an Indian Administrative Service [IAS] officer from Madhya Pradesh, I have been exposed to the bureaucracy right from my childhood. As the IAS is the backbone of the Indian bureaucracy, it was my privilege to have a personal connection with many of the ex-chief ministers including Uma Bharti and Babulal Gaur. Moreover I had an added advantage of knowing the leading industrialists of Madhya Pradesh as also the office bearers of national level Industry and Trade Associations.

I worked very actively with this team day and night to frame the new Industrial Policy. Everyone was charged up to become a game changer. Just to emphasise the intensity of positivity, I would like to narrate an incident here.

'I was at a wedding reception hosted by Arun Bhatnagar's [Former Secretary Government of India and Ex-Chairman *Prasar Bharti*] on the occasion of the marriage of his son at Bhopal, it was nearing midnight, when I met Raghav Chandra [IAS]. Just before in the morning of that day, a senior official of Vardhman Group had told me that they had intended to invest ₹1,000 crores [US$160 million] at Mandideep [Bhopal] on a new textile plant facility but now they are considering to shift this facility elsewhere as there is no proper response to their request from the State Government, hearing this from me, Raghav Chandra stopped having dinner, took out his mobile from his pocket, called up M A Khan, the Managing Director of Audyogik Vikas Nigam, Bhopal at half past midnight, told him to meet the concerned Vardhman people and report outcome of his discussions by evening. He was told how important it is for the government to get this investment because in the period 1998–2003 only ₹640 crores of investment had come to Madhya Pradesh. Needless to say with the dynamism of Raghav Chandra, the Vardhman Group agreed to invest in Bhopal. The plant's first unit came into operations in just 1½ years time.'

That incident was the beginning of my relationship with Raghav Chandra and proved to be a turning point for the growth of Madhya Pradesh.

From this day onwards we worked harder and harder to bring out the right kind of friendly investor policy. The policy was finally released after all stakeholders' consultations on 5th May 2004, 35 days after the deadline date but was made effective retrospectively from 1st April, 2004.

Gist of Industrial Promotion Policy 2004

Industrialisation of the state is only possible with excellent infrastructure and industry-friendly environment. The contribution of Madhya Pradesh to India's Gross Domestic Production [GDP] has not been commensurate with its rich and abundant natural resources. The Industrial Promotion Policy has accordingly been laid down along the lines of its industrially advanced neighbouring states. The new State Government desires that in future the rate of economic development of the state should be commensurate with other developed states. Therefore, to make Madhya Pradesh a prosperous state, it is essential that the rate of economic development should be increased. The achievement of the desired growth rate would only be possible when the development of industries and services sectors take place.

Inadequate infrastructure and power shortages during the last one-decade in the country led to a sharp decline in capital investment in the state, it hindered the pace of industrialisation and caused sickness in the industries. The Industrial Promotion Policy aims to address these issues to ensure – the development of quality infrastructure, to revive sick industries and provide maximum support, facilities and industry-friendly governance for industries.

The Industrial Policy launched in May 1994 was in force till 2003. The new Industrial Promotion Policy would be effective for the industries commencing commercial production on or after April 01, 2004. This policy would be effective from 1st April 2004 for a period of five years. Rules and procedures shall be modified in accordance with the new policy. However, capital investment made prior to this new policy shall still be governed by old rules and procedures prevailing at the time they were made.

Entrepreneurs, industrialists, industry associations, financial institutions and top officials of banks were consulted while preparing the draft of Industrial Promotion Policy. Their suggestions as well as ideas have been incorporated in a meaningful manner.

Employment generation is one of the major objectives of the new Industrial Promotion Policy. An initiative for this purpose has been taken in the state to launch new employment schemes for educated unemployed youth.

Objectives of Industrial Promotion Policy

- ✓ To make state administration industry friendly by simplifying rules and procedures.

- ✓ To accelerate the pace of industrialisation and make Madhya Pradesh industrially a leading state.
- ✓ To maximise employment prospects.
- ✓ To attract Non Resident Indians and foreign investments by developing world-class infrastructure.
- ✓ To create congenial environment for the development of small, medium and large industries.
- ✓ To ensure balanced regional development by generating employment in the non-farm sector.
- ✓ To chalk out special packages for removing industrial sickness.
- ✓ To integrate the different employment oriented schemes in order to provide employment opportunities on a sustainable basis.
- ✓ To rationalise commercial tax rates to make the state's industries competitive vis-à-vis industries in other states.
- ✓ To provide direction to industrialisation, keeping in view the available local resources and the existing industrial base.
- ✓ To ensure private sector participation in the state's industrialisation
- ✓ To financially strengthen the undertakings of the Department of Industries, enabling them to play a pivotal role in the promotion of industries.

Strategy for Industrial Promotion

- ✓ Providing incentives end facilities in the state to achieve objectives of Industrial Promotion Policy and ensuring effective implementation of planned strategy.
- ✓ An Employment Board has been set up for employment

generation under which policy for employment and self-employment schemes will be framed and monitored.

- ✓ Madhya Pradesh Trade and Investment Facilitation Corporation [TRIFAC] will be set up.
- ✓ In the process Of industrialisation maximum participation of private sector will be ensured.
- ✓ In order to promote investment, the rules of the business of the State Government would be amended. A Single-window system would be strengthened to make an effective and dynamic response by enacting the Industrial Facilitation Act.
- ✓ Technological up-gradation, modernisation and development of industrial units would be encouraged.
- ✓ Clusters of the industries would be identified and necessary steps will be taken to remove their deficiencies related to infrastructure, finance and marketing and technology.
- ✓ Financial concessions will be provided to promote small, medium and large Industries.
- ✓ Appropriate step for the development of the sectors of information technology, biotechnology, automobile, pharmaceutical, food processing, herbal industries will be taken by considering them as thrust sector industries.
- ✓ Rules for the rehabilitation of sick and closed industries will be simplified. A special package will be given for their promotion.

Proposed Action Plan – Reference to Strategy for Industrial Policy 2004

Industry friendly administration

Industry Advisory Council – An Industry Advisory Council headed by the Chief Minister would be constituted to give advice and suggestions to the Commerce, Industry and Employment Department for the industrialisation of the State.

Minister of Commerce, Industry and Employment – Vice Chairman

Members

Minister for Finance

Minister for Energy

Minister for Commercial Taxation

Minister for Housing and Environment

Chief Secretary

Principal Secretary to Chief Minister

Representatives of prominent industries associations of the state will be members.

Renowned economists, industrialists and other experts of national repute would be made special invitees/members of this council. The Principal Secretary Commerce, Industry and Employment would be its Member Secretary.

Constitution of Empowered Committees for Single Window Clearance

By amending the Rules of Business of the Government of Madhya Pradesh – to enact the Industrial Facilitation Act, empowered committees would be constituted. These committees would issue single-window clearances for industries and other investment projects. The empowered committees would have the powers to take required decisions within their jurisdiction for promoting time-bound investments.

A. District Level Empowered Committee for Investment Promotion

A District Level Empowered Committee headed by the Collector would issue clearances for projects involving investment up to ₹3 crores. General Manager, District Trade and Industry Centre would be its member-secretary. Senior officers of different concerning departments posted in the districts would be its members. The District Trade and Industry Centre would function as a secretariat of this committee.

B. State Level Empowered Committee for Investment Promotion

A State Level Empowered Committee headed by the Minister for Commerce, industry and Employment would issue clearances and give necessary direction/ orders for projects with investment above ₹3 crores [c. US$45,000] and up to ₹25 crores [c. US$4 million]. Managing Director, Madhya Pradesh Trade and investment Federation Corporation would be its member secretary while other members would include Principal Secretaries/Secretaries of concerning department Office of Madhya Pradesh Trade and Investment Facilitation Corporation would be the secretariat of this Committee.

C. Apex Level Empowered Committee for Investment Promotion

An Empowered Apex Level Committee headed by

the Chief Minister would issue clearances and issue guidelines and instructions for the projects with capital investment of over ₹25 crores. The Committee would also formulate strategies for investments.

This Committee would also take decisions about the implementation measures; proposed under the Industrial Promotion Policy and Action Plan such as rationalisation of taxes, facilities for mega projects and other related matters. This Committee would have the same powers as are delegated to Cabinet Committee on Economic Affairs, The Minister for Commerce. Industry and Employment will be Vice Chairman of the Committee while Minister for Finance, Minister for Commercial Taxation and Chief Secretary would be its members. Principal Secretary Commerce, Industry and Employment would be the Member Secretary. Depending on the subjects under consideration, Ministers of concerned departments would be specially invited as members of the committee, Madhya Pradesh Trade and Investment Facilitation Corporation [TRIFAC] would be the secretariat for the committee.

Commerce Industry and Employment Department would be the administrative department of the above said three committees. These committees would issue clearances/no objections. Under the Single-window system, clearances pertaining to Departments of Housing and Environment, Madhya Pradesh State Electricity Board, Food and Drugs Administration, Energy, Commercial Taxes, Revenue, Labour, Industry and Urban Administration would be issued in a time-bound manner. Madhya Pradesh Trade and Investment Facilitation Corporation [TRIFAC] would be constituted to promote investment and to advice Government in policy matters. This Corporation would be a restructured body of Madhya Pradesh Export Corporation and would function independently and would be the secretariat for implementing the Single-window System.

The industrial Promotion Policy and Action plan proposes measures to maximise employment opportunities, in order to achieve this; Madhya Pradesh *Rozgar Nirman* Board has been created for framing policy and monitoring the various employment and self-employment schemes.

Schemes envisaged to be implemented under the control and supervision of Madhya Pradesh *Rozgar Nirman* Board include

1. *Dindayal Rozgar Yojana*
2. *Pradhan Mantri Rozgar Yojana*
3. *Rani Durgavati Yojana*
4. *Cottage Industries*

After the cabinet approval of the new industrial policy 2004, the Chief Minister Uma Bharti in a function organised by FMPCCI at Bhopal, unveiled this policy to a packed house. The stage was now set for the implementation of the policy but the process to be followed was not yet clear. Meanwhile setting up of Trade and Facilitation Corporations Limited was initiated.

As far as I was concerned I thought my task was over but the fate had something more in offing for me, little did I know that my fascinating journey to get involved more actively with the government on Industrial promotion was about to unfold.

On morning hours of 11th July, 2004, my mobile started ringing and it was Bhopal Doordarshan [Government of India TV channel] at the other end inviting me for a debate at the studio on the growth of Madhya Pradesh. Few eminent panellists including Raghav Chandra [who has recently written a book, *The Scent of a Game,* on Tiger Conservation] who is currently Chairman National Highway Authority of India] were present.

I carried two documents for the debate, one was the 'Manufacturing Policy for India,' which I had submitted to Federation of Indian Chambers of Commerce and Industry, for an all India Competition. Incidentally, this policy received the award for being one of the top policy documents from FICCI, which had an Ex-Chief Justice of India as also a Former Cabinet Secretary and other eminent personalities on its jury.

The other document was the proposed vision of new Madhya Pradesh, which I had compiled by comparing Madhya Pradesh with other states.

When the panel discussions were over, it started to rain very heavily. Some of us waited at the balcony for the rains to stop. It is here that I gave Raghav Chandra, a suggestion that we should start a government-led growth drive in the state by enlisting the support of captains of industry, politicians [irrespective of their affiliations] and likeminded opinion leaders across the state nationally and globally. The state had to be trumpeted through multimedia, press and TV channels etc. He liked the idea and asked me to see him next morning with a two page note for putting it to the government. Next morning we discussed the conceptual business model for the Investors' meet and as the luck would have it, there was a Board meeting of MPSIDC/ TRIFAC on that day; he quickly prepared an additional agenda for the board meeting for its consideration. The

Board approved the idea and in a few days they offered me the job of an Advisor to MPSIDC and TRIFAC [Trade and Investment Facilitation Corporation] to implement the proposed business model.

I accepted the challenge, left my comfort zone and I joined MPSIDC/TRIFAC assignment on 28th July 2004 at 10.30 AM and left my first day in office at well past the midnight hour. My first day at the government job started with a 14 hours of very hard and challenging work. I never expected this kind of work load from the day one and this schedule continued till 19th August, 2004. The reason was that the Chief Minister Uma Bharti wanted to have one to one meeting with Infosys Chairman Narayan Murty and Wipro Chairman Azim Premji and a road show with the Karnataka Industrialists at Bengaluru. No one had a clue as to how to organise such an event on 18th/19th August, the notice was too short and the challenge much bigger.

Because of my back ground, I was told to immediately arrange for one to one meetings with the IT icons and to organise the road show with no indication of budget allocation though I knew that the department will fund it since it was a chief ministerial program.

The second challenge was to prepare an English translation of the Industrial Promotion Policy, which was in Hindi.

The third challenge was to at least make one catalogue that would show case Madhya Pradesh differently than other states especially depict Madhya Pradesh's cost advantages.

The fourth challenge was to organise a road show with the Karnataka Industrialists and Investors.

Initially I was all at sea – actually did not know how to complete these tasks.

In the case of the one-to-one meetings with Narayan Murty and Azim Premji, it was possible to have a direct contact with them through the government channels but senior officials in the CM's Secretariat were sceptical of approaching them, since it had become my responsibility. I could only wiggle out by succeeding.

At one level I contacted FICCI's office at New Delhi for their help, I must say that FICCI immediately responded and alerted their Bengaluru office to coordinate with Infosys and Wipro Chairman Offices. The indications were positive. As a backup arrangement I requested Karnataka Chamber's Secretary Ramappa to confirm FICCI State Council's feedback, once I got the confirmation, the Principal Secretary, Commerce and Industry and CM's office got in touch with them to fix venue and the timings. I was bit relieved as one major task was under control.

Since Raghav Chandra gave me full freedom to complete the tasks, I requested some MBA graduates to jointly translate the Hindi promotion policy into English, four MBAs worked on different chapters. Then I showed it to the Law Officer of MPSIDC for legally correct words. After that, it was shown to Raghav Chandra, who further corrected and approved it. Finally it took me 2–3 more days to read the English version to compare it word by word with the Hindi edition. This was all done in a great hurry – in government, one has to be absolutely sure about the wordings; my colleagues cautioned me of the repercussions if things go wrong. Well, to obviate this kind of eventuality, a rider was prominently put on the English version that in case of confusion or dispute, the Hindi version document would be treated as final. The English version was printed and was dispatched to Bengaluru along with the officials accompanying the Chief Minister's delegation. Task number two was achieved.

For finding the parameters of 'advantage Madhya Pradesh' required a much higher level of collective intelligence. I began talking to the industrial fraternity religiously on mobile every day, scanned through all the notes I had sent to the Government in last five years as Secretary of FMPCCI and tried to cross connect various inputs and ideas, almost for a week. The general perception was that Madhya Pradesh, being a land locked state, nothing much can be done to promote it and it was further stated that previous attempts to project Madhya Pradesh have failed. Kailash Chawla [Industry Minister] and Raghav Chandra were consulted daily to chalk out some salient features that would give an edge to Madhya Pradesh over other states. The churning of minds paid off and we created a land mark catalogue on Cost advantages of investing in Madhya Pradesh, which till now has basically remained the same. I remember Raghav Chandra complimenting me that, 'Pratap you have done what we expected from you and now you can relax a bit.'

The document went for printing on the night of 15th August. It was sent to Bengaluru by a personal air courier to reach in time. The entire exercise was done in three days. The 4th task with a dead line was to arrange a road show in Bengaluru on 18th August, 2004.

I spoke to the Secretary Ramappa of Karnataka Chamber on 3rd August, 2004. He assured me full support and promised a gathering of more than 200 Bengaluru based industrialists for Uma Bharti's road show.

I requested my previous organisation through my ex-colleague Meghna Ghosh to shoot out letters to the list of Bengaluru Industrialists they had with them, since she also knew Karnataka Chamber Secretary, the communication went on smoothly. Fortunately the FICCI Council Chairman at Bengaluru, S N Agarwal was also a leading member of Karnataka Chambers. We at TRIFAC made use of the combined list. Certainly we tried to contact everyone personally, and through emails and letters.

Our efforts paid off, she had a full house, eager to listen what she says. My regret was I could not attend the road show, as so many other things were pending at the back office level at Bhopal.

Her address at the Karnataka Chamber had a wide publicity in the press, the leading local and national newspapers covered the event. Economic Times and Business Standard prominently reported on her visits to Infosys and Wipro.

From her maiden effort to woo investors – especially the two ICONS, it was a span of 10 years before Infosys and Wipro decided to put their IT business at Indore in 2014.

This proved to her first and the last effort to interact with the investors as she resigned as Chief Minister on 23rd August 2004, paving the way for Babu Lal Gaur to become the next Chief Minister of Madhya Pradesh.

Babu Lal Gaur was sworn in as Chief Minister on 24th August, 2004, while Om Prakash Rawat [1977 Batch IAS] took over as the new Principal Secretary to the Chief Minister. There was a certain amount of lull at MPSIDC/TRIFAC since Babulal Gaur required some time to understand the new industrial policy but within MPSIDC and TRIFAC things started to become consolidated. Our core team of Vishwapati Trivedi, Raghav Chandra and J N Kansotiya, expanded with more core team members like R W Shrivastava, Ajay Choubey, J N Vyas, Satish Pendharker, Anil Rajoria and D S Chaturvedi. Each one of the new incumbent brought in complementary strengths to the core team. They were a fine blend of committed departmental officers with tremendous knowledge of ground realities at the grass root level.

After a very brief hectic period of July–August, I settled down to consolidate the recent gains and got busy in making an impactful presentation on the potential of Madhya Pradesh, its strengths and weaknesses [and converting weaknesses into strengths], like projecting Madhya Pradesh as a Logistic hub as it provided India wide connectivity that obviated its land locked geographical location.

As a prelude to carving out a new presentation, I got an opportunity to discuss our future course of action with Raghav Chandra who having studied at Harvard University, had the knack of leadership and management principles. Between ourselves we applied our minds using following concepts to bring about cultural change in the organisation to make the organisation investor friendly.

Concepts discussed

- *How to involve investors and other stakeholders in the industrialisation and growth of the state.*

We came to the conclusion that it can be best done by co-creating value on one to one basis focused on individual investor's needs through hardware, software, personal investor experiences, insights, business and social collaborations, use of professionals and data banks etc. With this mindset, the team was ready for embracing innovation process.

Innovation process

- Kaizen: It's more a frame of mind rather than a business process. Stakeholders should come to work each day, determined to become a little better at whatever it is, they are doing than they were doing a day before.
- Go to the source [question 'why' for a root cause analysis] Find the facts and do not rely on hearsay. Focus on defining right problems, simplify and actualise appropriate solution/solutions.
- Challenge: Problems are welcomed. To be viewed as pathway to improve performances, collaboration and coordination.
- Team Work and building trust in the team.

This means putting community's interest first vis-à-vis organisations and self interest by sharing knowledge and ideas honestly and synergising with complementary skills.

We prepared ground rules for working as a team by having following features in the team set up:

- Be a team player
- Demonstrate that you are working for other's interest as well as your own.
- Practice openness
- Be fair
- Speak your feeling
- Show consistency in the basic values that guide your decision making

- Maintain confidence
- Demonstrate competence
- Respect for other people. Different opinion must be expressed, but in a respectful way
- Brain storming ideas. Encouraging new ideas and brainstorming them for actualisation
- Collaboration and co-creation
- Practice Effective cultural and innovation habits such as
    1. Be proactive
    2. Keep the end in mind
    3. First thing first [Prioritise]
    4. Empathise
    5. Think win-win
    6. Synergise
    7. Serendipity
    8. See different, be different
    9. Exploration, inquisitiveness connecting the dots
    10. Sense, simplify and actualise
    11. Consider convergence of technologies
    12. Person context-value-roles-logic, SWOT, 80/20 rule as tools for innovation.
    13. Analysing feedbacks from the field and co-create
    14. Consider efficiency and effectiveness together

Match and merge innovation process, culture and habits with self awareness, collective awareness and eco awareness through open mind, open heart and open free will.

Meanwhile it was suggested by the Chief Secretary that FICCI's Secretary General Dr Amit Mitra should make a presentation before the Chief Minister and other Cabinet ministers and Principal Secretaries, describing the road map for growth of Madhya Pradesh and how FICCI and government can work together to achieve the objectives of the Industrial Promotion Policy.

Simultaneously TRIFAC had moved a proposal for holding an Investors' Summit at Bhopal with a proposed budget of ₹5 crores; few bureaucrats told me that no government will spend this kind of money on a *Tamasha* [Road Show], anyway we decided to wait till Dr Amit Mitra's presentation and proposal.

Dr Amit Mitra's presentation created waves in the audience. The Chief Minister Babulal Gaur directed TRIFAC at the venue itself to go ahead. Our proposal got a nod from the Finance Department with its characteristic style of trimming the budget by ₹1.5 crores and we were told to manage the activities within ₹3.5 crores.

We were informally told to first test the business model with the few activities and I am grateful to FICCI that they obliged us. The first two events at New Delhi and Mumbai were organised by FICCI through their own resources and it was done prior to signing of MOU between TRIFAC and FICCI. Dr Mahesh Reddy, the then Assistant Secretary General FICCI State Council was made the nodal officer from FICCI's side and I must say the whole TRIFAC team gelled very well with him. It was a 24 x 7 relationship for many years. We thank you Dr Reddy, for your valuable contribution to TRIFAC and Madhya Pradesh Government.

The first interaction to the Chief Minister with Delhi based investors was done at FICCI's auditorium to a jam packed house. The Central Minister for Commerce and Industry Kamalnath was also present. It is here that Babulal

Gaur showed his statesmanship by saying that we shall not allow politics to be a hindrance in Madhya Pradesh over growth related matters and I find the these sentiments still prevail between all political parties on this issue.

After the event in New Delhi, FICCI opened up its Madhya Pradesh State's Council at TRIFAC's premises with my ex-colleague Meghna Ghosh joining as Coordinator and head of FICCI'S State Council at Bhopal. She also became an active member of the core team. She was ably supported by another professional Maya Charde.

Ramesh Agarwal, the chairman of Bhasker Group accepted the role of President of FICCI'S State Council of Madhya Pradesh and played a very significant part towards the success of Global Investors' Summits. His personal rapport with most of the top Indian industrialists helped us to approach them with ease.

The next event was organised by FICCI on 7th May, 2005 at Trident Hotel, Mumbai for wooing the Mumbai Investors. Babulal Gaur was determined to have an impact at Mumbai by announcing at least one very big investment.

The big question was, how to get that one investment, which is at least of ₹10,000 crores [$1.5 billion]. TRIFAC knew that the BORL [Bharat Oman Refinery Limited] project is gathering dust for last 10 years. Vishwapati Trivedi and Raghav Chandra found an opportunity to rejig this project. The issue got serious consideration of the government between March–April 2005, various options were discussed and debated with BORL. We were at the threshold of arriving at the final outcome.

In the morning of 5th May, 2005, the issue was discussed with the Chief Minister, Chief Secretary, Principal Secretary of Commercial Taxes and Finance at Trident Hotel and a tentative draft was prepared for final discussions with the BORL CMD.

After the Indian Merchant Chamber event that evening, the BORL CMD was called for a make or break final decision and he came up with his senior officials and secretarial staff.

That night, Vishwapati Trivedi, Raghav Chandra, CMD of BORL and all of the team didn't sleep.

We finally drafted the MOU by 8 AM in the morning of 6th May, showed it to the Chief Minister and the Chief Secretary, and obtained their consent. The MOU was finally signed at 1.00 PM on 6th May, 2005 in presence of Babu Lal Gaur and thus began our crusade for garnering more investments for Madhya Pradesh.

Next day the MOU was the head line news in all leading national news papers and TV channels of India.

Indeed Madhya Pradesh had taken its first big leap towards shrugging off the BIMORU tag.

In Mumbai TRIFAC added up two more women members into the team Ms Mohini Bhadkamkar, Liaison Officer, MP Govt. and Dr Vajyanti Pandit, Director, FICCI, Mumbai.

We also tested the global summit model by arranging Investors' Meet at Singapore and Kuala Lumpur in the 3–4th week of May 2005. A small delegation comprising of the Chief Minister, Industry Minister, Principal Secretary, Commerce and Industry and MD TRIFAC addressed the investors at Singapore and Kuala Lumpur.

There were some one to one meetings with investors arranged through FICCI's network. I also happened to be there since my daughter Aarti was working at HP Singapore after completing her graduation [and also post graduation] from Nanyang Technological University on a Singapore Airline cum Singapore Government Scholarship. A half day trip was arranged for the delegation to Nanyang Technological University Innovation Centre that has been built up at the cost of Singapore $200 million, since I have been visiting Singapore very often during the 10 years of my daughter's stay, I could show the infrastructure development done at Singapore to the entire team.

June to November 2005 was a consolidation period for TRIFAC with inputs from FICCI. We did some hard work in developing infrastructure for auto cluster and waste disposal facility at Pithampur, which is spread over 5,000 hectares, housing large number of industrial units. The first green field SEZ of the country and Concor ICD [Internal container depot] at Indore became operational. Project on piped, water supply to Dewas Industrial estate from Narmada River was initiated. Thanks to Raghav Chandra's vision, dynamism and creativity all of them are now running successfully. He was a pioneer in the socio-economic development of the state and turned TRIFAC almost like a growth engine as if operating from the Chief Minister's Secretariat. As per the objectives of the Industrial Promotion Policy, the thrust was already on. TRIFAC collected all the relevant data from all the economic departments to make an integrated picture of Madhya Pradesh. The cultural mind set of the entire government began to change from power based to service based.

Lot of thinking process went into drafting departmental policies and once these policies were put into operations, positive results were visible.

These departments documented their own strengths

and published their own promotional material and conducted their own promotional events to highlight opportunities to the focused stakeholders.

With this kind of approach, the team work and the desire to excel grew among the employees of respective departments and they became motivated to be as competitive as some of the departments who were already excelling.

The awareness level regarding the departmental activities was greatly enhanced. The sector specific presentations gave them opportunity to show case their strengths and achievements to the outside world.

The creation and thought process of developing power point presentations enabled them to have clear vision and goals. They started realising that their effectiveness shall be benched marked by their efficiency and smartness to bring investments in their area of operations. It started to change the culture from one of administering to that of facilitating the work process for growth.

Since all the investments were monitored at the highest level in a time bound manner, departmental responsibilities and accountability increased many manifolds since they became answerable.

The MOU with FICCI was ready for signing but then suddenly the political scenario changed in the state and Babu Lal Gaur resigned as chief minister on 29.11.2005.

Shri Shivraj Singh assumed office as Chief Minister On 30th November, 2005 soon after a meeting between Shivraj Singh and Amit Mitra took place at Madhya Pradesh Bhawan, New Delhi in January, 2006 Dr Amit Mitra gave a road map of growth of Madhya Pradesh wherein FICCI could partner the Madhya Pradesh Government. It was a right move since FICCI'S partnership with Gujarat government was already yielding impressive results.

During this meeting Dr Amit Mitra suggested to the Chief Minister that to begin with, a conclave of Madhya Pradesh based Industrialists should be organised at Bhopal to felicitate and honour them with an idea to make them as brand Ambassadors for promoting Madhya Pradesh as an Industrial savvy State. The Chief Minister readily agreed.

After Shivraj Singh taking over as Chief Minister the political scenario got completely changed. Kailash Chawla did not find a place in the cabinet and Babulal Gaur became the new Industry Minister. TRIFAC earnestly began to work towards organising a conclave of MP based Industrialists at Bhopal.

On 27th March, 2006, the conclave was organised at Noor-us-Sabah Hotel, Bhopal. Most of the star investors of Madhya Pradesh attended. They were publicly honoured in front of a large audience and the press. They all spoke eloquently about Madhya Pradesh and responded positively to the appeal of the Chief Minister to act as brand Ambassadors of Madhya Pradesh. After the conclave, the Chief Minister had one to one meeting with each one of them and it's from here Shivraj Singh's journey for enlisting Madhya Pradesh as a developed state started to take shape. It may be mentioned here that before the conclave Rakesh Sahni took over from Vijay Singh as Chief Secretary on 20th February, 2006. We also had a change of guard at TRIFAC, in the second week of April when Praveen Garg took over from Raghav Chandra as Managing Director TRIFAC and MPSIDC

Now TRIFAC/MPSIDC had an entirely new set of

people at the helm of the affairs. The nature of the upper half of the core team has changed completely.

It was time for retrospection. Praveen Garg had his own strengths; he was the only CA among the Madhya Pradesh IAS Officers and therefore had a DNA of putting systems and infrastructure first before acting and leading. He led through analysis of the situation while Raghav Chandra acted more with dash and gut feeling. Praveen Garg got his confidence and commitment through analysis and as a CA, he quickly understood that he has landed up in a position where he can take the state forward economically with inclusive growth. He slowly but surely started building up the organisation by studying the core strengths of each of its team members and made them accountable in the areas of their strength to make whole team work by complimenting each other's strengths.

The first breakthrough for Praveen Garg after taking over as MD, TRIFAC came on 23rd May, 2006 when Hindalco signed an MOU for setting up an aluminium plant at Shahdol with a proposed investment of ₹17,000 crores [US$2.5 billion] The signing of the MOU was done in presence of the CM, Shivraj Singh at Noor-us-Sabah Hotel, Bhopal, with much fanfare.

The two big ticket investments of BORL and Hindalco [total ₹28,000 crores, over US$4 billion] gave a big boost to the moral of TRIFAC team and also increased the confidence of the Chief Minister that the approach towards attracting investments are going in the right direction.

We understood that the Investor focus and the change management can be continuously done by analysing the following trends.

- ✓ Demography
- ✓ Resources
- ✓ Market Perception
- ✓ New knowledge
- ✓ New technology and its convergence with other domains
- ✓ Studying government structures and policies to enable appropriate changes in them
- ✓ Process need
- ✓ Missing link
- ✓ Understanding reluctant investors
- ✓ Changes in logistic chain management
- ✓ Sustainable environment
- ✓ Unexpected occurrences
- ✓ Data mining
- ✓ Analytics
- ✓ Convergence of technologies.

We learnt that we need to create new business model by analysing 'Why, when, where, who, whom, what and how' with reference to the context and time. Our new business model should be such that it leads to

- ✓ Greater value addition at the least cost
- ✓ Reduced time cycle
- ✓ Provide brand value to TRIFAC and the government

This new thinking process allowed TRIFAC to evolve itself naturally. We realised that networking of people, communication as work, connecting and interlinking of related resources and processes are the keys for the success. Convergence of technologies can cut down the time needed to implement vision and objectives. We started practicing law of critical few, non linearity, creativity and innovation, which where the domains of corporate functioning. Scenario planning became the norm for each proactive activity. We learnt to act with flexibility, options and speed. We also learnt that to be globally competitive, one has to think globally and act locally and also think locally and act globally. Our team had become entirely interdependent and transparent and each one of us was working towards a common goal. In fact we had become hands on team, and each of its members was clear about her/his role.

We together also analysed the key drivers needed for promoting socio-economic growth of Madhya Pradesh. The major key drivers we found were as follows:

- ✓ A clear vision statement with strategies to achieve it
- ✓ Replicate successful practices and business models of other states
- ✓ Create brand ambassadors and press them into action to call upon other prospective investors to invest in Madhya Pradesh
- ✓ Rope in all national industry and Trade organisations.
- ✓ Network with foreign embassies and prominent industry associations in the world
- ✓ Bring outside consultants like Ernst & Young, Deloitte, and PricewaterhouseCoopers to provide outside perspectives
- ✓ Create government land banks for quick and easy allotments
- ✓ Make amendments in the labour policy to improve production
- ✓ Every economic wealth creation department must have a well defined policy

- ✓ Bring in Single-window system for ease of operation
- ✓ Digitise wherever possible
- ✓ Be IT/ICT [Information and Communications Technology] savvy
- ✓ Encourage facilitation role of the government
- ✓ Keep on evolving new opportunities

Global Investors' Summits as a Game Changer

The chief minister after being briefed by the Chief Secretary Rakesh Sahni and Dr Amit Mitra, was convinced about garnering investments into the state by using TRIFAC as his own Secretariat, he knew that only way to fuel growth is to pump in investments into the system, something, which the earlier governments neglected by trying to pay more attention to social engineering without focusing on attracting private investments and improving the enabling environment by creating right kind of infrastructure.

He understood and firmly believed that the private investment would only come if there is a 24 x 7 power supply, adequate availability of water with excellent mobility and communication within the state through good roads. This coupled with the inclusive growth by touching the lives of poor is the only way to bring prosperity in the state. Inclusive growth needed a thrust in the agriculture sector. The Chief Minister himself being a farmer wanted to make agriculture, a profitable business for the farmers.

TRIFAC's and FICCI's first presentation holistically depicted what was there in the Chief Minister's mind and he got the feel that this approach for Investors' meet will provide the necessary tool for him to accelerate the momentum of development in the state. It provided personal connectivity to him globally with right kind of people and has amicably branded the state by the impressive results achieved by his government. Investors also acted as brand ambassadors of Madhya Pradesh by sharing their pleasant experiences for being in Madhya Pradesh.

Between January–July, 2006, few more meetings of Dr Amit Mitra took place with the Chief Minister. The outcome was signing of the MOU for promoting Madhya Pradesh between Madhya Pradesh Government and FICCI on 6th August, 2006.

I must say for the period starting from August 2004 till the signing of the MOU, FICCI provided total support to TRIFAC without any financial consideration. During this period FICCI arranged 6–7 large events at their own cost.

The MOU envisaged an expenditure of ₹3.5 crores for promotional activities like domestic and foreign road shows, consultancy support from FICCI, E and Y for arranging of Global Investor's Summit in October, 2007 at either Bhopal or Indore. FICCI was to charge 8% of the amount that would be spent during this period as a Consultancy Fee.

FICCI was offered consultancy on 'Second Generation Development Road Map' for socio-economic growth of Madhya Pradesh; other than Industries and infrastructure, it was to offer advice on making agriculture a profitable business by finding innovative and disruptive solutions to the identified problems of agriculture; employment and marketing of new projects and improving the support system for MSMES.

A gala event was organised at the FICCI auditorium at New Delhi to welcome the Chief Minister. FICCI members from all over India were invited and indeed lot of leading industrialists like Sunil Bharti Mittal, Rajan Mittal, Singhania, Manoj Gaur, Rajendra Lodha, S P Oswal, Ravi Jhunjhunwala and Ramesh Agarwal, etc. attended the event.

An exhibition was also organised at venue showcasing the vision of Shivraj Singh at the entrance.

The Chief Minister officially unveiled the Industrial Promotion Policy 2004 [English version] at the inaugural event along with the signing of MOU.

The Chief Minister was cheered and applauded after the delivery of his maiden speech to the captains of Industry. Later on, he had one to one discussions with some of the prospective investors along with his team of officials.

After this event, TRIFAC got busy in creating a data base of the prospective investors and entered into serious interaction with the national Industry Associations and Chambers. We started attending their events to improve our networking with the prospective investors. We also interacted with the Embassies/High Commissions of USA, UK, Germany, Singapore, Netherland, Italy and Japan to put forward the presentation of Madhya Pradesh. This helped TRIFAC create global awareness about Madhya Pradesh. We were invited by the embassies and the high commissions to meet the prospective investors from the respective countries at New Delhi.

We also got in touch with World Trade Centre and Indian Merchant Chambers [IMC] at Mumbai.

The Chief Minister addressed the gathering of Mumbai based industrialists at IMC.

From here on the Chief Minister appeared very confident in his approach towards the corporate, the reluctance was gone forever and indeed this was reflected in his speech at the global. NRI meet address in January 2007 at Vigyan Bhawan, New Delhi. It was a highly emotional speech straight from the heart that impressed the large audience of NRIs from all over the world. He invited the NRIs to meet him at Khajuraho on 16th–17th January, 2007 to feel and experience Madhya Pradesh.

The Chief Secretary Rakesh Sahni, Principal Secretary Commerce and Industry O P Rawat [now Election Commissioner of India] and Praveen Garg were all present at the venue. They had a challenge to host an event for NRIs in next 7 days time.

Large number of NRIs attended that function along with the other important Industrialists of India and the journey of Shivraj Singh into the global arena and the corporate world got a kick start and from here onwards he grew immensely in stature.

This was the beginning of Madhya Pradesh's journey towards a better future. The evolution process had just begun and there was no looking back. All of us got into an achievement mode with hands on approach.

A series of road shows with the support of FICCI and Indian Embassies and High Commission were organised after the Khajuraho event leading to the first ever global investor summit to be held on 26–27th October. Between 10–20th May 2007, a delegation comprising of the Chief Minister, Industry Minister, senior government officials and important industrialists went on to promote of Madhya Pradesh at London, New York, Los Angeles, San Jose, Chicago and St Louis. Dr Deepak Kant Vyas with roots at Chhindwara in Madhya Pradesh, who resides at St Louis helped a great deal in organising the USA leg of the trip. Along with FICCI, he also supported the dialogue with the investors in the USA. Many Madhya Pradesh based Indians at these places enabled the delegation to create awareness among the investors, so much so that a Madhya Pradesh day was observed on 17th May at St Louis, Missouri. The Mayor of St Louis felicitated the Chief Minister who also rang the bell of the New York Trade Exchange for the morning start up of the exchange. The Indian Consul at San Francisco, Soumen Bagchi, who hails from Bhopal provided the extra mile value addition at San Jose and Los Angeles road shows. The high-powered Industrialists from Madhya Pradesh who accompanied the Chief Minister also played an important part in interacting with the prospective investors.

This tour was the first ever global awareness building attempt by the State Government on the business model of public private partnership [PPP model]. After each road show a one to one meeting was arranged with the interested investors.

The promotional give ways provided all the necessary details on opportunities in Madhya Pradesh and along with the facilitation mechanism of TRIFAC. An official presentation on Madhya Pradesh was followed by an 8 minute film with an appeal and direct questions and answer session with the Chief Minister, set the pace for each of the road shows. The Chief Minister in a similar fashion also visited Singapore and Malaysia.

Mumbai and Bangalore road shows were organised on 10th–11th August 2007 and 30th August, 2007 respectively. More than 4,000 invitations were sent by TRIFAC on behalf of the Chief Minister to prospective investors around the world for the first Global Investors Summit scheduled on 26th to 27th October 2007

TRIFAC General Manager J N Vyas facilitated direct telephone calls to important industrialists by the Chief Minister himself. These calls were backed up by request from the Principal Secretary, Commerce and Industry Avani Vaish [retired as Chief Secretary] and Praveen Garg, Dr Amit Mitra and Dr Mahesh Reddy also made personal calls to invite important investors.

The TRIFAC team was enthused since they had very capable as also considerate IAS officers like Rakesh Sahni, Avni Vaish and Praveen Garg.

They were deeply committed and involved in the whole process. Here I would quote my experience of interacting with Avani Vaish, who was at that time one of the senior most Principal Secretaries. He personally took me to each of the Principal Secretary of the participating department at Global Investors Summit to discuss their part in the final presentation on Madhya Pradesh. To facilitate this each department was directed by the Chief Secretary to prepare their own presentation on the opportunities available for investment in their respective departments. This gesture helped me in preparing the final presentation that had inputs from all the relevant departments; on another occasion I accompanied Avani Vaish to Japan to attend a meeting [23–27th July, 2007] about the Delhi–Mumbai Industrial Corridor [DMIC] project with the Japanese Government. We arrived at the Tokyo Hotel in the evening. At the reception, some of the state Chief Secretaries and other senior officials were standing at the lobby for an officially arranged tour of Tokyo city. Avani Vaish told me that Pratap, you go with them; don't worry about the check-in. I will do that for you. I do not need to go for the tour since I had seen

Tokyo many times. Without wasting time, I hurriedly got into the waiting bus.

I must say such acts by highly placed officers do bring in trust, loyalty and commitment. As I was from the corporate sector – this kind of approach makes you work even harder with responsibility.

Shivraj Singh gave a very personal and emotional speech at the first global investors' summit held at Indore on 26th and 27th October 2007. Here I quote some of the excerpts of his address.

'I am the Single-window.'

'You can walk into my office on Mondays and Tuesdays of every week between 11 AM–12 PM [noon] for any support you need from me in establishing your industry in Madhya Pradesh.'

'I shall be bringing Industrial Promotion mechanism under the Madhya Pradesh Public Service Guarantee Scheme.'

Apart from the overall presentation on 'Advantage Madhya Pradesh,' sector-wise presentation on opportunities in Power, Renewable Energy, IT/ICT, Education, Health, Mining, Tourism, and Infrastructure were organised.

Awareness on Advantage Madhya Pradesh had detailed various major important considerations for setting up businesses and investments in Madhya Pradesh [This was the first ever time the strengths of Madhya Pradesh were elaborated at one go].

The first ever Global Investor's Summit was attended by Kumar Manglam Birla, Anil Ambani, Rajinder Gupta, S P Oswal, Abhay Firodia, Sudhir Mehta, Sunny Gaur and Rajendra Lodha etc.

Each of them committed further investments in Madhya

Pradesh. In addition companies like BLA Power, ACC Cement, Satna Cement, Prism Cement, JP Rewa Cement, Bridgestone, Cummins Turbo Technologies, Liugong [India] Pvt. Ltd., Teva Pharma, Reliance Energy, NATRIP, Gail and some others promised to invest in Madhya Pradesh and inked MOUs with TRIFAC.

It must be acknowledged now [2015] that each one of the above did invest in Madhya Pradesh.

The global investors Summit 2007 was followed by regional investors meet at Jabalpur, Sagar and Gwalior particularly targeting the MSME, Food and Agro Processing.

The new Commerce and Industry and Commercial Tax Minister Jayant Malaiya who took over from Babulal Gaur on 27th August, 2007, personally met important Industrialists of India on one to one basis before the Indore Global Summit 2007 to ensure their presence at the Summit.

Later on Praveen Garg focused on implementation of MOU by contacting individual investor's on a regular basis. I used to accompany him on most of the occasions to Mumbai, Delhi, Bengaluru and other places. During our tours, we use to make it a point to meet more and more people with our presentation and promotional kit of catalogues and write ups.

The State Government realised the importance and impact of the investors' meet and recognised the pioneering work of TRIFAC team. In his address at the Indore Investors Summit Shivraj Singh publicly acknowledged the work of Praveen Garg saying that I know that Praveen along with his team has not slept for last two nights and TRIFAC has set up a new benchmark on its commitment towards my vision.

By end July, 2009, I thought I have done my job at

TRIFAC as an Advisor and I rejoined my earlier job as Secretary, Federation of Madhya Pradesh Chamber of Commerce and Industry, however I promised to Satya Prakash the then Additional Chief Secretary, Commerce and Industry as also Praveen Garg to be available whenever my services were required.

Seeing the result of Indore Investors' Summit the State Government decided to continue Investor's Summit model and has so far held similar investors' summits in 2010 [Khajuraho], 2012 [Indore] and 2014 [Indore] with different theme at each of these events.

I can say with confidence that the acceleration in socio economic growth between the years 2004–2008 created a favourable environment for improving the score card of BJP in Madhya Pradesh and they came back to power with a thumping majority in the year 2009.

As is it happens in bureaucracy, Praveen Garg after successfully navigating 4 years of assignment as Managing Director MPSIDC and TRIFAC was replaced by Anil Jain [now Advisor, Energy at *Niti Aayog*, New Delhi] with just a few months before the Khajuraho Summit of October 2010. Praveen Garg had left a very competent and able team of officers like R W Shrivastava, J N Vyas and Pendharkar to support him. Satya Prakash, ACS Commerce and Industry were already aware of the things to be done. Kailash Vijayvargiya was the new Commerce and Industry Minister. FICCI and Ernst &Young as usual partnered the government. In fact, Kailash Vijayvargiya played a leading and very important role in organising the Global Investors' Summit of 2010 and 2012 respectively. He ensured that Infosys and Wipro set up their IT Hubs at Indore.

Despite of my leaving TRIFAC, both Satya Prakash and

Anil Jain involved me in the process of the 2nd Global Investors' Summit 2010. I voluntarily contributed whenever a value addition was required or desired from me.

There were two such occasions worth a mention. One was on an inaugural road show at New Delhi on Agro vision of Madhya Pradesh as the main theme of Global Investor Summit No. 2, which laid emphasis on Madhya Pradesh's major strengths in agriculture and as per the wish of the Chief Minister; it was initiated to fulfil Chief Minister's desire to make agriculture a profitable venture. In fact the 2nd Global Summit was mainly dedicated to the 70% of the Madhya Pradesh's population engaged in farming and allied activities. The focus was to align farming with agro businesses to give farmers their due. It was an effort to bring the farmers the latest in technology to enhance their productivity. Lot of private sector players such as ITC, Rallies, Pepsi, Eicher, and Dawat Foods etc. got involved in their own way. The ITC model of E-Chaupal, [kisok] Pepsi's contract farming in the Ujjain/Indore region and Dawat Food's agriculture extension work for rice became the models to be emulated, the world over in the wealth creation for farmers especially in the developing countries. These models augmented the wealth generation process in the real time. It gave the Chief Minister an opportunity to learn from the world class companies the art of wealth creation in agriculture. At this point of time, I just wish to say that this global summit increased the awareness level of the entire farming community and it was a pleasure to design a presentation for achieving Chief Minister's Dream project of making farming a profitable venture. The Global Investors Summit synchronised the efforts of farmers, Government, Corporate entities and banks with stream of ideas flowing in. The second occasion was when the duo wanted my assistance in organising the Europe tour that was scheduled in June 2010, what happened that at the last moment the Indian Embassies in Netherland, Italy and Germany expressed their inability to help effectively, since according to them, it was not the right time to visit these countries. As it is, organising a foreign visit for a Chief Minister requires a very elaborate and lengthy process and needs approval of government of India on various issues. The entire exercise was done and the delegation was to leave in 2–3 weeks time. This news from the embassies disturbed the bureaucracy and required channelising the program from other reputed sources as well. It is here that my personal networks in Netherland, Germany and Italy provided the necessary confidence to host the events in these countries. Here I must thank my ex-colleague and a very dear friend Sanjiv Mehta, the present Chairman and Managing Director of Unilever India and the Executive Vice President South Asia, who was at that time, the head of Unilever for the Gulf and Africa. He responded quickly to my SOS because of which the tour was a success.

This was the time, I had the opportunity to interact directly with the Chief Minister, Industry Minister, senior bureaucrats and corporate leaders for a period of two weeks of the Europe tour. It was a great experience in learning, exchange of ideas, self awareness, collective awareness and eco awareness. It certainly expanded my vision and I am quite sure, it expanded the vision of the Chief Minister as well as we visited and interacted with people and companies who were working together to improve farm productivity, infrastructure development and renewable energy especially relating to farming processes. Ideas stick in the mind and then in the course of time multiply and connect with your own environment. That's how new creative ideas and innovations take place.

During the long sojourn of Global Investor Summits the State Government was able to reach to practically all the who's who of Indian Corporate majors among them had been Mukesh Ambani, Cyrus Mistry, Kumar Mangalam Birla, Anil Ambani, Gautam Adani, Narayan Murty, Azim Premji, Swati Piramal, Sashi Ruia, Adi Godrej, Rajinder Gupta and S P Oswal etc. I am happy to say that all of them had put their investments in Madhya Pradesh.

I am confident that Shivraj Singh must have enjoyed his life's journey through the Global Summit's of 2007, 2010, 2012 and 2014 that has brought laurels to the state of Madhya Pradesh. I am both lucky and proud to be a member of the pioneering team that started the journey and wish his new team comprising of Industry Minister Yashodhara Raje Scindia, Antony DeSa, Iqbal Singh Bains, Mohammed Suleman, S K Mishra, Kanta Rao, Vivek Agarwal, Hariranjan Rao and D P Ahuja; who are carrying on the baton since the Global Summit 2014. Not forgetting the Additional Chief Secretary P K Das and Arun Bhatt who admirably managed the Global Investor Summit 2012.

Program anchors also play an important role. My old childhood friend Sukanya Balakrishnan, the famous Doordarshan English newsreader did her job with grace and precision. Her father and my father were colleagues in the IAS. Her husband was Secretary to the Government of India as well but her heart, I knew always belonged to Madhya Pradesh, she researched the Madhya Pradesh script to compile an excellent presentation at the first Global Summit 2007. Sukanya delivered it with personal energy and professional aplomb.

The media played a vital role in making people aware on the impressive growth of Madhya Pradesh. In particular Shashikant Trivedi, a journalist from *Business Standard* promptly did a very thoughtful and factual report on the development of Madhya Pradesh.

Now it's time for the Government to rethink the business model of Global Investors' Summit as much has changed since 2007, the state and nation has to evolve new paradigms for the growth of people keeping the global perspectives in mind – it needs to think both locally and globally. The State Government has to now leverage the convergence of technologies and use of collective awareness and new processes by bringing the technology and people together by modifying the Global Investor Summit model or by totally creating a new model. We shall soon discuss the immense possibilities that will make it happen.

To my mind, the most important priority for Madhya Pradesh now is to link education and skills to enhance the overall productivity of the state. If we neglect this area, we are destined for failure in a digital knowledge economy.

3

HIDDEN BENEFITS OF GLOBAL INVESTORS' SUMMITS

The idea of Global Investors' Summit was mooted somewhere in the year 2004 and as we look back at the beginning of the year 2016 and analyse the impact it created in government working, lot of new advantages and benefits have emerged, which were not thought of when this business model was conceived for garnering both public and private investments from around the world. The business model was highly successful in attracting investments into Madhya Pradesh but has also brought in a significant cultural and mind set change in the thinking of the state government. This new gaming business model has brought kudos to the State Government and the Chief Minister.

- ✓ The biggest impact has been that it made government as a facilitator for public service through sensitivity and proactive responsiveness towards satisfying the needs of common people. The service guarantee scheme acted as a catalyst in augmenting this process.

- ✓ It integrated the socio economic growth opportunities present in various departments under one platform, i.e. TRIFAC.
- ✓ There is a competitiveness among all government departments to showcase their achievements during the sector wise presentations and promote opportunities of growth present in their areas to investor's assembled at one place.

Since State Global Investors' Summit is held every two years, the whole process of showcasing has become dynamic by incorporating changes happening in market place and the society.

'The freshness in State Government's approach is distinctly visible.'

- ✓ Each department came out with its own set of rules and policies by learning from the Madhya Pradesh Industrial Promotion Policy 2004. The 2004 Policy was the first attempt to integrate all the growth opportunities under one policy document for growth.
- ✓ Learning from its content depicting vision for the whole state, the other departments chalked out their own specific policies for promoting their own department to the outside world.
- ✓ The increased awareness of various issues led to creative and innovative solutions to create an enabling environment and awareness among investors to invest in Madhya Pradesh.
- ✓ Each of the department started thinking about 'Ease of operation,' for people to interact by using the principle of simplicity through the use of technology

and increasing the awareness in the government employees that they exists to provide services to people rather than providing only regulation and control.

✓ TRIFAC created more interaction and communication among departments to understand the wholeness of the overall shared Vision.

✓ TRIFAC was perceived more like the Secretariat of Chief Minister's office by the bureaucracy and anything coming out of TRIFAC and connected to State Global Summit was dealt on priority basis with full responsibility and accountability even at the district levels.

This happened because TRIFAC has a dynamic monitoring system and all activities relating to investments are communicated to the Chief Minister on regular basis stipulating the actions required.

- The seriousness and concern shown on issues connected with State Global Investor's Summit at the empowered committee of Chief Minister and also that of the Chief Secretary and in front of other senior people brings in a peer pressure on each department to act speedily to resolve issues.
- In fact the monitoring model has now been applied successfully for making agriculture as a profitable business. The approach to achieve this vision also uses many aspects of State Global Investors' Business model.
- The result and outcomes of making agriculture as profitable business are there for everybody to see.
- The State Global Investors' Summits present the

score card of its performance backed up by the statistics and data to the general public and also enlists the future course of action.

- Global Investor's Summit has extended government's networking globally, which is benefitting the government in various ways.
- Global Investor's Summit generates employment, skill generation and entrepreneurial ideas and innovation. Both government and corporate teams learn from each other.

It is evident from the above that the Global Investor's Summit model has revolutionised the working of the Madhya Pradesh Government and is primarily responsible for taking out the *Bimarou* tag from Madhya Pradesh.

It has an interesting analogy to the Global Quality movement through Kaizen, TQM and 6 sigma, they no doubt brought in quality revolution in the world but the success of quality movement was attributed to the rare insight provided by the late management guru, the great Peter Drucker, who said that no doubt the quality has improved substantially but the real reason for the success of the quality movement and its improvement has been the rigorous professional and human interactions that took place to achieve the thought processes of implementing Kaizen, TQM and Six Sigma.

So now the Global Investors' Summit is the new tool the governments can emulate to become creative and innovative.

In a nutshell, State Global Investors' Summits fostered creativity as also innovation in government work. To understand the effectiveness of the model, one must be aware of the process of generating creativity with innovation.

Stretching your awareness is the key to creativity. It is the skill to look at the same thing everyone else does yet have the ability to see things differently as well as find hidden connections to create something new.

Innovation is thinking up something new to make complicated things simple. Innovation is 'doing new things.'

Some people have ideas; few carry them into the world of action and make them happen. They are innovative leaders. They have rightly imagined, moreover perceived ideas with timely precision. Certainly Shivraj Singh belongs to that league of innovative leaders.

Creativity and innovations require perceiving the problems correctly and differently by doing both convergent and divergent thinking at the same time, then integrating them for solutions through both the right and left brains i.e. logic and emotions. This kind of thinking allows people to find remote associations, furthermore connect them to provide right answers as well as redefine and reframe perspectives.

Leaders are able to synergise the complementary skills of individuals in a team for implementing innovative ideas.

The innovative Global Investor's Summit model was able to break the mental lock and block of bureaucracy regarding the operation and governance of government through control, regulation and administration.

The model cajoled them to look differently at the problems and find solutions through the public participation. This realisation made them think differently.

It propelled the bureaucracy towards transformational thinking [and leap frog] from incremental thinking. It knocked down the maze walls to allow for new model of inclusive growth and governance.

Through State Global Investor's Summits the Chief Minister and his government has learned to harness the collective brain power of large number of people [crowd sourcing] that has made Madhya Pradesh globally visible and competitive. The model provided

- ✓ Participative leadership with shared vision.
- ✓ Task focus.
- ✓ Harnessing of complementary strengths and skills.
- ✓ Problem Solving and subsequent evolutionary process.
- ✓ Using 360° communication with transparency.
- ✓ Proactive attitude, responsibility and accountability.
- ✓ Peer pressure to act because of the public glare.

State Global Investor's Summits is a creativity and innovation leadership tool in government work for bringing 'happiness to people,' which is the main task of any government. This tool is slowly transforming human resources into human capital in Madhya Pradesh.

In their book *Reinventing the Corporation,,* John Naisbitt and Patricia Aburdene observe that organisations are experimenting to act differently in many ways to produce desired results in the shortest possible time with least effort and resources by employing right kind of human capital. The State Global Investor's Summit Model just does that by intuitive abilities, flexibility and adaptability in a participative manner [*Sab ka sath, sab ka vikas*]. It has become a proven tool to tackle volatility, complexity, ambiguity and uncertainty.

According to emotional intelligence guru, Harvard professor Daniel Goleman, for a process to be successful it should be derived both from the head and the heart i.e.

by using both logic and the emotions – harmonising both of them is essential.

The government thinking should have both efficiency and effectiveness and should make use of both soft and hard thinking.

Right brain [Soft thinking]	**Left brain [Hard thinking]**
Metaphor	Logic
Dream	Reasoning
Humour	Precision
Ambiguity	Consistency
Plenty	Work
Approximation	Reality
Paradox	Exactness
Diffuse	Focused
Hunch and gut feeling	Analytical

Governments can identify disruptive opportunities by focussing on these basics.

- ✓ Clarity on the jobs to be done.
- ✓ Analysing the current and the future tradeoffs [through scenario planning].
- ✓ A shift from output to outcome.
- ✓ Provide autonomy and empowerment to innovate through budgetary provisions.

A few disruptive opportunities that are present in today's scenario are listed here.

Defense	Using unmanned drones for doing multiple jobs, at the fraction of the traditional operational costs.

Intelligence	Data mining, use of open services of knowledge, cloud computing search engines and advance analytics for quantum leaps in socio-economic growth.
Prize Competition	Involve people through crowd sourcing.
Education	Online education to supplement class room education.

We are now in the era of creative economy. The primary, secondary and tertiary economics are merging into a borderless creative economy; each one is getting more and more integrated with the other. Creative economy requires synergy between them by embracing convergence of technologies. It is here that the State Global Investor's Summit model could be a game changer to the people of Madhya Pradesh and in addition can show the right path to governments around the world.

These are the ways to proceed with the model.

- ✓ Contemplate new management structure.
- ✓ Understand the role of government in a creative economy.
- ✓ Strategic harnessing of opportunities.
- ✓ Create clusters of innovations.
- ✓ Bring positivity and diversity in government structure by inducting competent people from outside for specific assignments.
- ✓ Get people on to the team who can stick their neck out.
- ✓ Follow transparent and open government system.
- ✓ Convert human resources into human capital.

- ✓ Creativity and innovation require governments and organisations to become knowledge producers, researchers and learning seekers.
- ✓ An innovative government ensures balance between efficiency and effectiveness.
- ✓ IT/ITES/ICT/Mobile phones to be used as major tools for fostering innovations.
- ✓ Government innovations require new policy frame works and strategies.

Innovative Governance seeks to develop a value addition in the work processes and services that are more responsive to the community requirements. Also by the address of expectations through trust – built among community members through transparency with the ability to achieve targeted outcomes.

Innovative government would require reengineering its model of governance to infuse efficiency and effectiveness at the same time in its cadres with stakeholders in the community. This can ensure goals – the vision can be attained at the lowest cost in the shortest possible time with the least issues through a Single-window approach.

Modern technologies have brought unprecedented changes in the culture and life styles of the people because of which the traditional role of governments, which was attributed to four governance pillars: legislation and justice, law and enforcement, holding power, protection and security and regulating rights among its people and other stakeholders has undergone significant changes. Consequently to meet the rise of creative dynamic economy in place of the combination of primary, secondary and tertiary economies, the governance system needs to become creative and innovative. This is the biggest challenge for the governments around the world. They have to manage both efficiency and effectiveness at the same time by assuming new roles quickly.

Modern governments have to be responsible to lead the common people towards development by an improvement of people's life styles as well as provide them with social and humanitarian care.

So their success is now dependent on how much their services are valuable and effective. New technologies have entered into government portfolios such as 'Quality of Services, people satisfaction and happiness for all,' which are all influenced by the environment. Under the circumstances the governments have to reinvent, reengineer and continuously evolve by infusing and embedding creativity and innovations in the governance systems.

This means the governments have to be continuously aware of the changes taking place in the environment and society in order to be creative and innovative to provide value addition all the time in its work processes and services in a professional and precise manner.

Also this requires a digitised single-window process that considers human emotions and cultural norms within the community to fulfil people's expectations to get desired outcomes through trust and transparency.

An innovative government has the ability to achieve a balance between efficiency, effectiveness and technology. It diligently seeks learning, innovation and creativity as tools for accomplishing goals and objectives that are the part of its grand vision. This is done by making dynamic and innovative policies that encompasses four main elements individuals, communities, processes and technologies. New governance structure is derived from the policy themes. The success to attain maximum value addition depends upon the quality of its human resources that brings both focus and diversity into the system.

Innovative governments seeks to achieve integration, coherence and harmony between its different departments and units to make efficient and effective delivery through single-window by the use of convergence of technologies through a single-window process by providing ease of operation in delivering required results. The single-window process does the overall representation of all government agencies, such an approach leads to hassle free accelerated growth at a fraction of costs.

Our experience of Madhya Pradesh Global Investors' Summits has opened up a new model of growth and governance by reengineering and reinventing the government machinery to deliver required results.

In the Madhya Pradesh Global Investment Summit Model, TRIFAC is inadvertently making the State Government creative and innovative as it is enabling various departments to restructure themselves to be creative and innovative by peer pressure. It ensures government agencies are knowledge producing, research and learning organisations. The global summit model is preparing them to meet global challenges and radical changes in the government work and is inspiring the concept of formal, informal and social learning at individual, collective and organisation levels.

The Global Summit investment policies and strategies show case the efforts of government and investor's towards the inclusive growth of the state. Inviting the participation of public through crowd sourcing fuelled by prize competition IT/ITES/ICT/Mobile technologies are enabling the government to provide open data, big data and cloud computing to empower people with disruptive ideas and networking of collective human resources to accelerate the inclusive growth of its people. This leads to 'open innovation' as a governance tool. This way the government becomes more transparent and open.

Government offices are no longer seen as back offices for implementation of policies, but as a front offices dealing proactively with citizens, reaching out to them and providing services they need at their places. This requires government departments to focus more on human capital development and thus contribute to the progress of their people.

With the advent of Madhya Pradesh Industrial promotion policy 2004, there were host of departmental policies put forward by all major departments for attracting investment and participation through Public Private Partnerships with corresponding rules and regulations. Departmental websites began showing the friendly attitude of the bureaucracy. The effect was contagious, things began to change and happen. Energy department came up with separate Wind Power Policy, Solar Policy, Bio Mass Policy, Small Hydro Power Policy, MOU Policy 2012, MP [Investment in power generation projects] – Policy 2012 and PPA – Policy 2012 with vision statements. The individual department and websites were made user friendly and are updated regularly.

The Madhya Pradesh Industrial Promotion Policy 2004 was amended and revised in 2007, 2010, 2012 and 2014 keeping in view the changes in economic scenario and investor's feedback and to include the best practices of other states to be ahead in providing incentives and ease of operation in comparison to the other states.

To make people happy, service guarantee scheme under a specific time period limit was introduced. At present the schemes caters to more than 160 listed activities with grievance mechanisms.

The CAGR rate of GSDP jumped from 3% in 1999–2004, to more than 10% from 2011 onwards.

Not many people know that it happened because of the State Global Summits, which is being used as tool for transforming the government with its inherent properties and process of generating creativity and innovations and we all know disruptive changes bring magical results.

New creativity and innovation ideas for enhancing the power of State Global Investor's Summits:

- ✓ Enter into partnership with Global and nationally reputed institutions.
- ✓ Have a conclave of evangelists, entrepreneurs along with the display of innovative products and projects.
- ✓ A conclave for state and national governments, economists from globally reputed universities, World Bank, ADB, IMF to explain and showcase the Madhya Pradesh model of creative and innovative governance triggered by the initiation of State Global Investors Summits.

The world at large will be greatly benefited by this idea as it will touch poor people and in fact all of us would benefit from the power of State Global Investors' Summit model.

New ideas and road ahead for Global Investor Summit to foster wealth generation:

New Ideas

- ✓ Make YouTube/Facebook/Twitter as part of various processes
- ✓ Services of experienced and competent retired personnel are taken for running finishing schools and skill development schemes
- ✓ Innovation school
- ✓ Crowd Sourcing platforms
- ✓ Kiosk for digitisation
- ✓ Multi language centre
- ✓ Driving Schools
- ✓ Executive Yoga Centres
- ✓ Recycling business
- ✓ Global Manpower generating institutions
- ✓ Community policing
- ✓ Medical Tourism
- ✓ Use roads as pathways for solar power, lying of cables and gas pipe lines and social forestry and horticulture, and logistics, to create funds for road development and facilitating employment
- ✓ Get FDI by making people globally aware of Madhya Pradesh growth model and its achievements.
- ✓ Use surplus capacities of private engineering colleges for ITIs
- ✓ Women life coaches and knowledge SHG's at Village in the PPP mode

Road ahead

The Global Investors Summits so far have been successful in meeting its objectives as has been stipulated and described in detail in previous pages. The GDP growth has been consistently above 10% in last 4 years and is expected to grow at the CAGR of 12–13% per annum for at least next five years because of the investments already made and also, which are currently in the pipe line.

Therefore it is the right time to ponder over the steps and direction on which the growth strategy should be mooted through Global Investor Summits in next 10 years. In order to grow at 12–13 beyond next 5 years certain directional changes have to be incorporated in the Global Investors Summit frame work by analysing the future global scenario.

Various research studies have identified the following trends.

- ✓ By 2030, 65% of the people shall live in urban areas.
- ✓ Biotech, ICT, IT/ITES, Nano, Micro, Laser, Robotics and Space technologies shall have convergence and would determine future life style and economics.
- ✓ Eco awareness shall open up opportunities in waste recycling.
- ✓ Knowledge and awareness would be the key for future employment and employment trends will shift from natural resources to knowledge industries.
- ✓ The new accelerated system for wealth creation will be largely dependent on exchange of data, Information and Knowledge, data mining and convergence of technologies. No new knowledge exchanged, no new wealth gained.

- ✓ Bureaucracies to ease of operation and market socialism.
- ✓ Empowering of women, individuals and teams by continuous retraining and development through self learning.
- ✓ Better health care.
- ✓ More and more jobs shall be available in service sector.
- ✓ Innovations and R&D shall be the socio economic game changers.

Each of the above trends and opportunities would require a separate strategy for inviting investment in a particular domain.

One lesson for an integrated approach to growth of Madhya Pradesh can be drawn from the development of cities such as Mumbai, Delhi and NCR, Pune, Bengaluru, Hyderabad, Chennai, Ahmedabad and Kolkata, as they have been the prime movers and growth engines in the development of their respective states and India at large.

Therefore to provide impetus to growth in Madhya Pradesh, it must consider marketing important cities of Madhya Pradesh by developing them based on the global opportunities cited above.

Recent signing of MOU's on metro rail projects at Bhopal and Indore with JICA, Japan is a welcome step in the right direction. The state government is already in touch with South Korean companies for setting up innovation centres at Bhopal and Indore.

Most of the times, there is an all round criticism on foreign tours by Chief Minister's delegation. Getting Foreign Direct Investment [FDI] has a long gestation period and takes long time. It may be mentioned here that some of the foreign companies like John Deere, Force Mann and Caparo did make investments in Madhya Pradesh after the one to one contact of the Chief Minister with them during the foreign tours. The other advantage of these tours, is the global perception acquired by the Chief Minister and his team by personally seeing what is happening outside India, the innovation centres of Samsung at Seoul and Unilever at Rotterdam and the green houses and solar energy installations, at Munich [Germany], these are some of the examples that benefitted Madhya Pradesh by incorporating some of these processes to make a 'SWARNIM' Madhya Pradesh.

In order to effectively use new opportunities, we need to improve our cities by making people smart through smart systems and provide an enabling environment based on each city's strength so that each city is able to harness opportunities offered based on their culture, knowledge and strengths.

To achieve socio economic growth of the 7 major cities of Madhya Pradesh namely Indore, Bhopal, Jabalpur, Gwalior, Ujjain, Sagar and Satna a frame work is required for creating an enabling environment for each of these cities, so that each city becomes a wealth creation power house. Activities and areas for investment needs to be identified first and then projects and business models may be proposed to the investors in next Madhya Pradesh Global Investors Summit scheduled in October, 2016 [Good luck to the Chief Minister Shivraj Singh, Yashodhara Raje Scindia, Mohammed Suleman and their team]. Chief Secretary Antony DeSa would be lucky to be a part of this event as he would be retiring on 31st October 2016 but Madhya Pradesh would be fortunate to use his vast experience to make the event fruitful.

4

THE IMPACT OF GLOBAL INVESTORS' SUMMIT ON THE CHIEF MINISTER SHIVRAJ SINGH FOR MAKING AGRICULTURE A PROFITABLE BUSINESS

To make agriculture a profitable venture, the credit goes entirely to Shivraj Singh who led from the front and had rare insights about farming and agriculture at the last mile level, he being a farmer himself had fully understood the problems of the farmers and was deeply committed to resolve their difficulties.

He has ensured 10 hours x 7 power supply, irrigation, loan at zero per cent rate and use of technology to make land holding below 2 hectares profitable. He facilitated construction of E-*chaupals* for procurement and knowledge dissipation, diversification of cropping patterns, and value addition at each step of farming and storage of farm yields as per HACCP standards.

Shivraj Singh has learnt his leadership lessons right

from his early childhood by his concern for others – to make him fight for social justice. Before becoming Chief Minister on 30th November 2005, he already had a long political leadership experience having served as General Secretary of the youth wing of BJP, and had become an MLA in 1990 and since 1991 remained as Member of Parliament till elevation as Chief Minister of Madhya Pradesh in 2005. His active participation in politics just before the emergency days landed him in jail as a MISA detainee. In jail he was greatly influenced by reading Tilak's *Gita* and studying Sant Gyaneshwar, both of these made a lasting impact on his personality. He was fortunate to have been associated with leaders like Atal Bihari Vajpayee, Kushabhau Thakre, Lal Krishna Advani and Sunder Lal Patwa.

He created mass appeal by doing pad yatras [leadership by wandering around] in rural areas and was popularly known as *pav-pav wale Bhaiya* [brother travelling on foot], as Chief Minister his image got changed to that of a *mama* [Maternal uncle] to large number of women and children when he initiated many welfare schemes for them. He has a Bachelor's degree in Arts in which he earned a first division, in spite of being actively involved with politics and public life.

As a farmer with considerable amount of rural cultural knowledge and his day to day experience with the real issues of the farmers, he was determined to do something for the farmers and realise his ambition to make agriculture as a profitable business. His experience on agriculture was also enriched by being member of the parliamentary committee on agriculture that helped him develop global, national and local perspectives on agriculture issues.

Now was the time for him as a Chief Minister to fulfil his dreams by acting in the right direction by connecting agriculture, to the other economic sectors to make Madhya Pradesh a developed state. His political acumen and leadership provided an anchor to just do that but differently from other politicians, economists and bureaucrats and as the track record shows, he led from the front in the right direction.

Global Investors' Summit as a tool for making Agriculture as a profitable business

While other states and people around the world were busy in the economic growth, Shivraj Singh believed that to make people happy; requires a process that is a notch above the economic growth because when we talk of inclusive economic growth, it means that it makes all strata of society sustainable.

Shivraj Singh had a conviction and belief that agriculture can be made a profitable business and his confidence was based upon the hands on experience he had gained as a farmer. He knew agriculture in and out and knew the problems and the solutions as well. Now as a Chief Minister he had the necessary infrastructure and power to do exactly that. His strong desire and the will to provide meaningful happy life was about to be fulfilled to a large extent, what he needed was a necessary participatory roles of each of the relevant stakeholders.

The challenge was to bring political leaders, bureaucrats, investors, entrepreneurs, farmers, and press and PR agencies together under one platform to fulfil his long cherished dreams.

The partnership with FICCI, E&Y and professionals gave him the outside perspectives and the thought process as to what knowledge people [other than the government machinery] can provide for value addition in meeting his agriculture vision.

As has been said TRIFAC with the support of FICCI, E&Y large corporations and investor's presented a workable business model to the Chief Minister who was leading from the front.

The business model galvanised and synchronised the work of the Energy, Irrigation, *Panchayats*, Warehousing and Agriculture departments, etc. The business model also provided linkages and connectivity to E-business, Banks and Financial Institutions, etc.

The focused attention to this agriculture business model got a kick start after the *Kissan Panchayat* held in August, 2006.

The phenomenal results are there for everybody to see. The achievements are stupendous and remarkable. Its success goes to Shivraj Singh because he believed that agriculture is Madhya Pradesh's main strength with unlimited potential. He firmly believed that the previous governments have neglected the agriculture totally. What it has done to Madhya Pradesh's economy is very hard to believe but then the figures speak for themselves. From 2007–2014, the percentage of the GSDP share of Agriculture has jumped from 22% to 30%. This changed scenario happened because Shivraj created an enabling environment by taking the following steps.

- ✓ Ensuring 10 hours of power per day continuously for irrigation through the separate feeders to operate irrigation pumps.

- ✓ Making Madhya Pradesh a power surplus state.
- ✓ Banking loan reduced from the prevailing rate of interest of 16% in 2004 to zero interest in 2014.
- ✓ Giving farmers an enhanced maximum support price and providing insurance cover subsidy.
- ✓ Encouraging diversification of crops.
- ✓ Providing funds for construction of spot dams and dug wells.
- ✓ Increasing net cultivable area.
- ✓ Ensuring timely supply of quality seeds, pesticides and fertilisers.

Now is the time to look into as to how it actually touched farmer's lives and aspirations.

- ✓ Majority of homes have electricity at home and the television penetration has jumped from 20% to 44% in last 10 years.
- ✓ The Gross State Domestic Product [GSDP] has grown at more than 9% consistently since 2009–2010 and most of it has grown on account of agriculture. The share of GDP in agriculture is growing at the rate of more than 20% during last four years [2011–2015] thereby increasing the share of agriculture GDP to 30% [22% in 2004], clearly indicating the entrepreneurship and effort put forward by MP farmers in an enabling environment.
- ✓ The fishery production is up from 66,000 MT in 2004 to more than 1 lakh tonnes in 2014.
- ✓ Land under cultivation grew by 21% in last 10 years.
- ✓ Loans to farm sector has gone up from ₹3,300 crores in 2006 to more than ₹11,200 crores in 2014.

- ✓ Power supply to agriculture went up by 87% in the period 2009-2014.
- ✓ Waiting time at *mandies* has been cut down drastically with the introduction of digital technology.
- ✓ Farmers are updated *through* mobile apps.
- ✓ *Krishi Vikas* Centres have been energised. [Agriculture Development Centres]
- ✓ Easy availability of fertilisers and seeds.
- ✓ Expanded warehousing facilities.
- ✓ Improved rural network of roads.
- ✓ Increased sense of security to women and children through welfare schemes.
- ✓ Focus on organic farming [India's 40% organic food production takes place in MP].
- ✓ Improved productivity in the area of animal husbandry, fisheries and poultry.
- ✓ Relief given to farmers in times of natural calamities.
    - ▸ To my mind no chief minister till to date has paid such as apt attention to improve the life of farmers and the people living in the rural areas.
- ✓ An empowered *Krishi* [Agriculture] Cabinet committee headed by Chief Minister was formed to oversee the process with the powers of the cabinet to take speedy decisions.

Madhya Pradesh is now leading the way into next agriculture revolution. At the time of 1st agriculture revolution in the 1960s, the states in India grew at 5% GSDP in agriculture and now with almost 20% GSDP CAGR consistently for last 4 years, Madhya Pradesh is becoming a global entity in the field of Agriculture. Credit must be given to R Parasuram [former Chief Secretary] and M M Upadhyay [former Production Commissioner] for relentlessly pursuing the chief minister's dream.

This is not the end of the road for Madhya Pradesh, still lot has to be done consistently to show the world that agriculture can also be an alternative driving force to make poor people empowered and happy. Our quest shall continue consistently in future to provide a road map to the world for eradication of poverty and enlighten governments on the art of making people happy.

The world needs to know that the empowered humanity can do more than the knowledge gathered at Harvard, Stanford and Cambridge. Shivraj Singh has already shown the way to harness the potential of poor people by providing enabling environment. The World Bank, The IMF and The ADB have to learn this governance model from Shivraj Singh. Here are the results.

- ✓ Farmers are able to grow on average 50–60 quintal of paddy in 1.5 acre of farm.
- ✓ Sprinklers use only 50% of water to that of a conventional system and hence more water is available for irrigation. Also sprinklers as per the study done by IIM Indore improves the productivity of the crop by 20–30% depending upon the crop sown. Sprinkler usages by most farmers are improving the farm productivity.
- ✓ Nearly 200 villages have been converted into Yantradoot grams [Mechanised Villages]. There are 286 mechanised equipment hiring centres in the state and 450 new ones are being established.
- ✓ MP has become a number one state in the production of quality seeds with annual production of 43.95 lakh

quintals followed by AP [40.04 lakh], UP [37.08 lakh], Maharashtra [10.1 lakh], and Gujarat [5.5 lakh] in the year 2013.

- ✓ The wheat production grew from 72.08 lakh MT in 2008 to 177.25 lakh MT in the year 2015.
- ✓ The state jumped from 13th position in 2005 to fourth position in 2009 in terms of agriculture produce.
- ✓ In 2012 and 2013, 2014 and 2015 MP was adjudged as one of the top state in agriculture by Government of India in the grain production category.
- ✓ The storage capacity at Warehouses has gone up from 9 million tonnes to 15 million tonnes in the period 2011–2014. In addition lot of private warehouses has been set up because of a new warehousing policy. The team led by Warehousing Corporation MD Shiv Shekhar Shukla must be given due credit for this achievement.

5

THE INFRASTRUCTURE REVOLUTION OF MADHYA PRADESH

It is a well known fact that investor's flock at places where they are welcomed; treated with respect and are provided with an enabling environment and infrastructure that includes power, roads, adequate water, air and rail connectivity. The enabling environment also includes availability of land at a low cost, peaceful environment, non parochial culture backed up by excellent administration and law and order coupled with state of art education and research institutes and greening of society.

At TRIFAC we tried to analyse the Madhya Pradesh's position on the above matrix and consciously made policy suggestions, goals and vision to translate potential and possibilities that Madhya Pradesh was endowed with. The effect was contagious and was visible all over the state. To develop participative culture the chief minister mooted a Madhya Pradesh song.

Our campaign to attract investors had given them promise of deliverables in the shortest possible time. This was acknowledged by leading industrialists of India such as Kumar Manglam Birla, Anil Ambani, Adi Godrej, Sunil Bharti Mittal and others. The fact of the matter is that TATA, Birla, ITC, Reliance, Eicher, ITC, P&G, Godrej, Vardhman, Trident, Videocon, Rio Tinto and Force Mann, etc. all have strong presence in Madhya Pradesh. The heads of leading organisations have become our brand ambassadors and they invariably talk about the political will, friendly bureaucracy and enabling environment by citing their own experiences.

Let us now look as to how Madhya Pradesh created infrastructural necessities for investment to flow in the state. The developmental process for creating infrastructure has given substantial employment to people and the government expenditure and investments in infrastructure development in last 10 years is estimated to be US$15 billion [More than ₹1 lakh crores].

POWER

The state has added millions of new consumers. With increased power availability it has enhanced the rural economy by way of providing power to cottage and village industries.

Government of Madhya Pradesh [GoMP] is working relentlessly to achieve his vision of 'Power for all.' The availability of power in Madhya Pradesh has increased by 240% compared to the year 2003. Under the Atal Jyoti Abhiyan, quality power is being supplied to non-agricultural consumers 24 x 7 and over 10 hours to agriculture consumers. Total 48,00 MW power was available in the state in 2003, which has increased to 15,500 MW. Arrangements of adequate power availability have been made as per demand till the year 2022.

Energy Department has increased transmission capacity by 33% during last four years. This capacity was 34,232 MVA in the year 2010–2011, which has risen to 45,457 MVA in year 2014–2015. During this period, 50 new ultra high tension power sub stations were set up. In 2003, transmission capacity in the state was 3890 MW, which has gone up to 12,600 MW in 2015.

In the year 2003, electricity consumers were 63 lakh 96 thousand, which has increased up to about 1,15,00,000 [2015]. Power distribution companies have paid special attention to quality improvement in rural areas. During last four years, numbers of transformers have increased by 74%. There were 2,67,000 transformers as on March 2011, which have increased to 4,65,000 [2015].

EASE OF DOING BUSINESS IN POWER COMPANIES

The three power distribution companies have started providing high tension power connections online. With this, applicants for high tension connections need not visit the offices of the company. Arrangements for payment against connection have also been made online. Number of prescribed documents for obtaining connection has also been reduced from 14 to 2. For up to 33 KV connections, facility of inspection by third party has been made, instead of obtaining charging permission from electricity inspectors.

REDUCTION IN INTRANSMISSION LOSSES

Transmission losses in the state have been reduced to 2.82% which is the lowest in the country. Along with feeder separation work, widespread infrastructure projects are also being undertaken under power sector reforms in the state. During these 4 years, length of 11 KV lines has been increased by 55%. As on March 2015, total length of 11 KV lines was 3,13,000 kilometres, whereas it was only 2,02,000 kilometres as on March 2011.

RECOGNITION FOR OUTSTANDING WORK

Madhya Pradesh has been conferred awards in five different categories for outstanding works in New and Renewable Energy Sector in the year 2014–2015. The awards were given away by Union Minister of State for New and Renewable Energy, Piyush Goyal to Principal Secretary New and Renewable Energy, Malay Shrivastava.

The excellent works for which Madhya Pradesh has been awarded include establishment of maximum capacity grid based solar power projects during year 2014–2015. Madhya Pradesh stood second in the country in this category. Madhya Pradesh stood second for establishing maximum capacity grid-based wind power projects during year 2014–2015 and second in the category of maximum capacity grid-based power projects of all techniques during the same year.

OTHER ACHIEVEMENTS

The Government of Madhya Pradesh [GoMP] has taken note of the growing recognition for impact of climate changes at the local, national and global levels and taking lead on this, the GoMP has decided to tap its vast potential for Solar energy. The state of Madhya Pradesh is endowed with high solar radiation with around 300 days of clear sun and offers good sites with potential of more than 5.5 kWh/sqm/day for installation of Solar based projects.

With an aim to promote the generation of renewable energy, Madhya Pradesh is set to get world's largest solar power station in Rewa district with a total solar installed capacity of 750 MW The plant will start generating solar energy by March 2017.

Solar energy capacity in the state was 2 MW in March 2012, which has increased to 354 MW in year 2014 and 466 MW in March 2015. This capacity is expected to rise to 2,000 MW by March 31, 2017.

The present installed capacity of wind power is about 450 MW and the biomass and small hydro power installed capacity is approximately 100 MW

Roads

Madhya Pradesh was known for its bad roads. In fact in 2004, there were hardly any roads. Now Madhya Pradesh has extensive network of national and state highways, and district and village roads.

20 national highways with cumulative length of about 5.000 kilometre pass through Madhya Pradesh. The state also has about 8.750 kilometre of State Highways. The central geographic location makes Madhya Pradesh an ideal state for making logistic hubs that can provide economies of scale for distribution of goods throughout India. Multinational FMCG, P&G operates all its all India distribution from Bhopal.

In the last 10 years, nearly ₹35,000 crores have been

spent on development by the State Government to either construct or improve the roads, a very challenging task and the state government deserves kudos for it. Further improvement of networking of roads and its maintenance is underway. The business model of building BOT roads under PPP has been highly successful in Madhya Pradesh and has been a major source of providing employment to unskilled people.

Water Management

Large investments have been made for completing the unfinished irrigation projects, making new dug wells, irrigation pumps, micro irrigation, and interlinking of rivers. The high points have been the interlinking of Narmada and Kshipra river at Ujjaini Village in Indore district at a cost of ₹432 crores and water supply from Narmada river at Nemavar to Dewas by 128 kilometres long pipe line.

Future planning and reservation for water supply to Industries from Narmada has already been done.

The irrigated land area is now 36 lakh-hectares against 7.5 lakhs in 2004, resulting in magical increase in agriculture productivity, paving way for using surplus yields for Food and Agro processing industries. Now is the time for investors to set up their agro based units in Madhya Pradesh.

Industrial Infrastructure

Government Land banks of 26,000 hectares spread over the state is available for industrial use.

Innovation in Law and Order

As per records and statistics available in the year 2000, nearly 13% all India crimes on women and children have taken place in Madhya Pradesh alone. This has come down to 7.3% in 2011. The overall crime rate has also declined considerably. The decadal crime rate [per lakh of population] has shot up in all states between 2003–2012, the rate of growth has been Maharashtra at 45%, Rajasthan 78%, Delhi 81%, as against a low rate of growth at 15.7% in Madhya Pradesh.

State Government subscribes to the view that development and security are two faces of same coin. Perception of safety and security is very important to attract large scale investments. People feel secure only when they believe that government agencies would be readily available at their service in case of emergency. State has statutory responsibility to establish the State control room under section 41-C of code of Criminal Procedure.

In emergency, people are generally made to contact local police station or police officers to get police services. But contacting appropriate police station or right police officer is always a challenge in the present police station centric system. Hence state government has approved setting up of a state level dial 100 based police control room cum command and coordination centre at Bhopal to empower, people to connect to police and get police assistance anytime, anywhere at very short 'response time.' This service will be comparable to the legendary 911 service of the United State of America.

Madhya Pradesh police is soon going to set up centralised state level dial 100 control room cum command centre in Bhopal for police related emergencies and other services to help people in distress. The proposed centre will be equipped with latest technological tools like GIS MAP for whole state, CAD [Computer aided dispatch] and GPS enabled 1,000 first response vehicles to attend to handle public distress calls for services. First response vehicles will be deployed across the State. Around 6,000 to 8,000 police personnel will be dedicated for the service equipped with wireless Radios, CUG GSM connectivity and other model gadgets and weaponry.

As soon as a person makes a call on '100'number, it will be received at the centre by well trained staff who will take necessary person specific details, incident details, and location details. Besides computer systems will also validate the same on the basis of CLI database, GIS MAP, Vehicle database, and other information available in public domain.

The trained dispatcher would immediately dispatch nearest available one or more well equipped first response vehicle. Each vehicle will be monitored and tracked through the GPS based AVLS equipment fitted in the vehicle. Calls by women will be attended by lady staff.

Each call and each activity would be recorded on centre's voice logger and web portal of activities.

Once the first response staff reaches the destination, it will take necessary action including taking down FIR on the spot as per 'standard operating procedure' of the centre. After the action is taken, state PCR's dedicated feedback team will contact the call maker and victim about the quality and satisfaction of the service provided by the police teams. Voice logger would ensure post incidence appraisal and third party audit of all call related information. There is also provision to facilitate the caller to be able to talk to senior officer of concerned District using three party conferencing and video conferencing.

It will also be integrated with other existing emergency number like Ambulance, Fire; Women help line and Child help line, etc. This software based system would also be used for preparing daily patrolling plan, picket duty, point duty, traffic management and better management of recourses in general.

When the project becomes fully operational, no complainant would be required to visit police station. Police would itself reach the person calling on '100' number. This dream project of MP Government would be a 'Game Changer' in true sense and path maker for others.

In the next phase video feed of CCTV surveillance cameras, being installed at 2,000 locations across the State will be available in the control room. The proposed 'command and central' room would have CCTV surveillance data feed for 30 days. It will help in identifying the culprits and nab the offenders. The electronic data would be trustworthy evidence to get conviction and protect the innocent in the Court of law.

6

SHIVRAJ SINGH – AN INNOVATIVE LEADER

Shivraj Singh is undoubtedly treading Madhya Pradesh on the developmental path by creating enabling environment encompassing creativity and innovations in the process of governance. Madhya Pradesh under his leadership has won the prestigious United Nations Award at New York in June 2012 for Madhya Pradesh Public Service Guarantee Act under the UN's category of improving the delivery of Public Services. The state has been for last 4 years is getting the National Award on agriculture – *Krishi Karman* Award, for achieving new milestones in agriculture. The state is achieving the highest agriculture GDP growth on an average of 20% consistently for last four years. Madhya Pradesh has also received the best tourism state award many times.

Paradigm shifting innovations take place when an innovative leader acts with the will, desire and determination to create and transform, and not follow historical norms; she or he had looked at the same issue differently to derive alternative perspectives.

Just as the way Steve Jobs changed the way we now live globally as one village through convergence of technologies, Shivraj Singh has done a socio-political change in a *Bimarou* [undeveloped] state like Madhya Pradesh that has now become a model of Governance, leadership, management and convergence of technologies to empower people to live with a growth oriented progressive mind set. He has succeeded in kindling hopes of better lives in 72 million people of Madhya Pradesh by applying both the head and the heart for the welfare of the people of Madhya Pradesh.

These very significant achievements and milestones are not possible without enabling environment that requires proactive attitude, resolve and commitment of the top leadership. It also requires a challenge to benefit the poorest by the monitoring of last mile initiatives and taking everybody along on a journey to fulfil the aspirations of people, making the people happy through a common shared vision.

All this needs extraordinary levels of institutional leadership with the astuteness in the fields, of management, leadership and governance. Shivraj Singh has delivered what he thought, he can deliver. His ground level achievements have put Madhya Pradesh on a growth path and for that the generations to come would be thankful to him.

He proactively reached out to people of all shades through community *panchayats*, empathised with them at *panchayat* gatherings, took their suggestions, tried to resolve their problems at the spot itself by agreeing on solutions. For issues requiring further deep thinking, action plans were made in a time bound manner with monitoring mechanisms.

His human approach, patience and ability to stay calm helped him connect with people. The holding of *Panchayats* [community gatherings] enabled him to reach out directly to the last mile grass root people, giving him first hand information on the ground zero.

His art of governance through Community *Panchayats* is truly unique and strikes a chord with all sections of the society. It was not the top down bureaucratic approach but involved participation of grass root people to participate in decision making in their own specific areas. This strategy successfully engaged the people to evolve and become productive by helping themselves. The government by offering quick solutions created an enabling environment so people can do their activities without hassles. The government truly became a facilitator by empowering people by making things simpler. To a large extent this made coercion approach of the bureaucracy to administer and control by citing rules [and ruling by power] less prevalent.

The *panchayat* strategy was social engineering at its best, which had both efficiency and effectiveness that kept people engaged and involved. These *Panchayats* were policies in action.

At the time of writing this book 37 such Panchayats have been held encompassing different strata of the society.

The first such *panchayat* was held for women on 30th July, 2006. It was a great success and instantly connected Shivraj Singh to families across the state because every family is centred on a mother or wife and if she is happy, the family becomes happy.

The first *panchayat* was followed by many more such *panchayats* such as farmers, tribal, MSMEs, scheduled castes, artisans, fishermen, *Mandi hammals*, and street vendors, etc.

Most of the *'panchayats'* were held at Chief Minister official residence. A large section of relevant departmental officers along with ministers of respective departments used to be present during the Chief Minister's address and interaction with audience. The transportation and hospitality for the *panchayat* stakeholders were arranged by the government, free of cost.

The decisions taken at the venue were notified immediately, budgetary sanctions were obtained from the finance department on the spot and the required actions by the concerned department/departments were stipulated right there. Issues that required more information and decision making parameters, dead lines were set for resolving the problems. The *panchayats* were held from morning till evening and the Chief Minister did lot of empathetic listening at these *panchayats* that touched people emotionally and connected them to Shivraj Singh at heart to heart level and that's a hall mark of any political leader – lead both logically and emotionally.

Overtime, these deliberations at *panchayats* became part of state policies and road map for making action plans.

The *panchayat* model enabled Shivraj Singh to touch upon each aspects of leadership i.e.

- Information and data
- Knowledge
- Skills
- Insights
- Vision
- Wisdom

All this he could muster at one platform, in a simplified and dignified manner. He interconnected everybody present at the *panchayats* because it directly touched their lives and that too instantaneously and that made people 'HAPPY AND SATISFIED.'

The *panchayat* model is also a brilliant tool to execute another principle of governance and management i.e. plan, lead, organise, and control [PLOC] with appropriate monitoring mechanisms for feedback and corrective actions.

The governance system via *panchayat* route motivated people to become more productive rather than depending upon doles and subsidies. It empowered people to act positively to help themselves.

It is during these *panchayats,* he got rare insights to the human problems and ways to create solutions. If the problems are solved, people are happier. Here are the few examples and lessons from these *panchayats.*

The women and child social issues like gender bias, women empowerment, education of girl child were tackled innovatively. Shivraj Singh related to each of the woman and child by projecting himself as Mama [Maternal Uncle] of each family. In his addresses, he assured the girls not to worry about their education, marriage and deliveries. He said that as a Mama, he would fulfil these responsibilities. It was a master stroke in establishing emotional links with the families through the rigorous implementation of schemes of *'Ladli Laxmi Yojna,' 'Kanya Dan Yojna'* and *'Janani Suraksha Yojna.'* These grass-root schemes, visibly saw him living up the image of *mama* [uncle: mother's brother] – a *mama,* who really took care of underprivileged women and children.

The free distribution of bicycle to girls allowed them to

attend schools regularly. Each morning, you see the girls cycling down to their schools on rural roads wearing their free school uniforms and carrying their books.

The Ladli Laxmi Yojna is now being implemented nationally. Under this scheme the Madhya Pradesh Government buys ₹6,000 worth of Saving Certificates each year for a period of 5 years when the girl is born. A certain amount of money is given for her education and later on at the age of 21 years, if she does not get married before the age of 18 years, a lump sum amount of ₹1.18 lakh is given to her.

So far since 2011 more than 21 lakh [2.1 million] girls have been benefitted by this scheme. The objective of this scheme is to facilitate girl child's education and empowering her with social security.

The *Kanyadan* Scheme. In India when the girl gets married, culturally she as the bride is given many household articles and money as a token of love as also to provide socio-economic security to the bride. At the time of marriage the government chips in its share of '*Kanyadan*' by giving ₹15,000 as cash for the marriage expenses. This scheme is applicable to all communities and religions. Till now nearly 3.57 lakh girls have benefitted from this scheme.

Under the *Janani Suraksha Yojna*, a woman in labour is taken by government transport to the government hospital for a free delivery. In last five years more than 64,00,000 babies have been delivered at the government hospitals. In 2003, the institutional deliveries were just 26%, but now the figure has sky rocketed to 84%. To facilitate deliveries at government hospitals around the state nearly 9,000 new beds have been increased in last few years. Cash amount of ₹1,400 is given to the mother at the time of leaving the hospital.

Another initiative have been to provide 50% reservation to the women at *panchayat* and local body elections, now there are more than 15 lakh [1.5 million] women who are elected and associated with these bodies by fighting elections.

There are many more such schemes which have been evolved through holding of '*panchayats*' at the chief minister's residence. These '*panchayats*' are the living examples of 'Crowd-Sourcing' at its best where more or less instantaneous solutions were provided to various sections of the society. The public commitment at the venue becomes the challenge and had put peer pressure on the bureaucracy to perform and deliver. It has changed the mindset of bureaucracy to perform under full public glare with media watching.

Shivraj Singh has proved that if there is a will, there is a way. Through the '*panchayat* route' and using '*panchayat*' as a tool, he has been able to solve simple and complex issues as well, with relative ease by taking various stakeholders into confidence and developing a participatory approach to carve out acceptable solutions.

The State Government's governance mantra may be summarised in analysing the information and data, knowledge, skills, insights, foresight and wisdom by following the principles of vision, commitment, transparency and innovative governance and management as well. Government effectiveness goes up if the people participate in the process of governance. A government must be able to create an enabling environment by empowering people and involving them in the process of governance by implementing their valued suggestions for greater productivity.

State Global Investors' Summit joined the government, other stakeholders, implementers and partners to work together to execute the vision, seamlessly.

The untold story of Madhya Pradesh reveals as to how other governments can emulate the Madhya Pradesh model of growth for progress and happiness for its people and connect them globally. It acts as a compass to navigate the existing scenario to a new paradigm shifting scenario that makes life easy and happy even at the grass root levels.

The model will enable governments, businesses and social enterprises etc. to align themselves to a new era of life styles that encourages creativity and innovations at all levels. This model is an exercise in gravity shifting.

The model emphasises it is not enough to have one big idea alone. It takes a series of innovative solutions to the entrenched problems to make a breakthrough and transform an eco system. The model has woven technology, people transformation, policy change and innovation in government design.

It has brought together the best of businesses and best of social innovations by keeping economic and social growth at the centre of businesses, and let them grow together.

At deeper level it changes the mind sets of the people.

The global investor summits acted as a tool for him to transform Madhya Pradesh. The story is big and never researched and revealed earlier by any one and needs reader's attention. This is how it unfolded and made every stakeholder to participate in the holistic development of Madhya Pradesh. The Global Investors' Summit connected everybody to the process of resurrecting new vibrant

Madhya Pradesh by creating a right vision for Madhya Pradesh where Shivraj Singh's experience as a farmer has lifted the GSDP of State Agriculture to double digit consistently for last 4 years [2011–2015].

I remember the FICCI presentation that Dr Amit Mitra gave to him that January 16th evening 2006 at MP Bhawan, New Delhi, at the end of the presentation, Shivraj Singh told Dr Amit Mitra that please see that the proposed Global Investors Summit lays emphasis on inclusive growth particularly taking care of farmers growth, so that the Agriculture becomes a profitable business.

From here onwards, FICCI always prioritised agriculture throughout its partnership with the State Government that lasted till the 2nd Global Investors' Summit at Khajuraho in 2010.

An awareness campaign was done by FICCI for the Agro based Industries and industrialists of India; various best practices in agriculture were brought to the notice of the Chief Minister. Lot of interactions between the Chief Minister and the agro industrialists took place; one of the positive outcomes was introduction of Basmati Rice in the Narmada belt of Hoshangabad district and adjoining districts based on the business model of contract farming. The business model created a win-win situation for both farmers and the initiator company Dawat Foods. Now more and more rice companies have installed their rice mills at Mandideep and the farmer's income has greatly enhanced by adoption of modern technology in farming. Similarly Pepsi has entered into contract farming for potatoes in Indore–Ujjain belt, and another successful business model. ITC's E-*Chaupal* has become a game changer in procurement of wheat and more and more companies like Hindustan

Unilever and Reliance started processing wheat from Madhya Pradesh. ITC has expanded its E-*chaupal* model successfully to many countries.

The involvement and intervention created a mind set for introducing best practices and technology into farm sector for improving the productivity. The Chief Minister also became self aware of various issues, which need to be tackled at the government's level. Shivraj Singh connected the missing links and data beautifully and holistically to make agriculture a profitable business.

FICCI, E & Y and TRIFAC interconnected various departmental visions towards the objectives of garnering investments and especially to make agriculture a profitable business. The presentations envisioned future processes and targets to achieve the Chief Minister's dreams.

The holistic presentation on Madhya Pradesh set the direction, pace, and road map for the growth of Madhya Pradesh.

Ideas multiplied and the chief minister extended the concept of Global Investor's Summit for conducting focused '*panchayats*' for various sections of society. The first such *panchayat* was held at the Chief Minister's residence for women on 30th July, 2006. This *panchayat* was hugely successful with large number of women attending it. Through this *panchayat* they got an opportunity to express their views directly with the chief minister, his cabinet colleagues and the senior officials present at the *panchayat*. Many of the solutions were found on the spot and instructions given to the relevant departments. The minutes of the deliberation were properly recorded for the necessary action which was personally monitored by the Chief Minister, concerned departmental minister and the

Chief Secretary. Shivraj Singh discovered a new model of governance where he out scored everyone in the country and made his model different from Gujarat by introducing issue based ' *panchayats*' for different sections of the society. He developed a new model of directly connecting with the masses and the beneficiaries. His motto was to make **people happy** by providing solutions to the problems of various sections of the society.

Shivraj may not have been to Harvard but he has tons of experience on human connectivity. To understand the model just think of 'QUIT INDIA' Visionary slogan that empowered each Indian to work in unison for a powerful vision by collectively acting as us. It was an exercise in raising awareness, commitment and coordination and empowered people to full fill their role to make India independent, the slogan had clarity of purpose. Similarly each of the 37 '*Panchayats*' held so far had clarity of vision and a road map for each stakeholder in meeting the vision.

At the *panchayat* itself several policy making ideas were generated and Ladli Laxmi Yojna was one of them. From here onwards Shivraj's image from *pav-pav wala bhaiya* was transformed into being *mama* [maternal uncle] of all girls in Madhya Pradesh.

Holding '*panchayats*' was a brilliant thought of Shivraj Singh, which perhaps emanated from the learning of global investor's summit model.

The second such '*panchayat*' was organised for farmers wherein Shivraj Singh explained about his dream regarding making agriculture as a profitable business. Problems, ideas and suggestions poured in and they were discussed thread bare. Some decisions were taken on the spot itself and there were many more to be taken soon to make farmers happy.

Focused *Panchayats* have already touched up farm labourer, MSME entrepreneurs, construction workers, rickshaw pullers, street vendors, artisans, bamboo craftsmen, etc. and it must be said that everyone got something out of these *'panchayat'* deliberations.

Analysis shows that his new governance model is based upon the Alchemy of I, You, We and Us, which has six different parameters for connectivity between people that is synchronised through a purpose. In the case of *'Panchayats'* it was to make 'people happy.' It struck a chord with the people. In the Alchemy governance model, I is the one who becomes self aware first, then he makes the other person self aware and once the communication begins to spread, it makes 'We' aware of the common shared vision of making everybody happy. When 'We' works towards the shared vision with eco awareness, the results starts flowing in the connectivity loop. It allows people to follow the human qualities of open mind, open heart and open free will. This approach as Shivraj Singh learnt from his *'Panchayats'* provided him the emotional connect with people at will.

This new leadership model can be remembered as the 3A + 3F model.

3A stands for

Self Awareness
Collective Awareness
Eco Awareness

This awareness is created in this way.

I in me – imprinted memories and past events in the brain

I in you, we and Us [We becomes Us when people collectively work towards achieving shared vision] – Flexible beliefs, feeling

I in Now – Freedom of choice

And when everyone becomes aware of the vision, they follow the participatory approach to meet the vision through 3F.

Feeling
Freedom of choice
Flexible beliefs

The *'Panchayats'* joined the people of Madhya Pradesh and created a road map for making 'people happy' through participatory approach between all concerned departments in the government to work towards a common vision. This approach has minimised the departmental barriers to a great extent. The policy of each department exemplifies the direction it has to follow for collective gain.

The *'panchayat'* model is a new successful experiment in democratic governance and is a self evolving and dynamic model that provides meaning to the work that people do.

In this model politician, bureaucrats and related people work together to get results. The British dominated model of top down governance is slowly being replaced through the cultural change the *'panchayat'* governance system is ushering towards the speedier development of Madhya Pradesh.

When this model is backed by the positive attitude, authenticity transparency and analysis, it becomes a very powerful tool for taking effective actions. It collectively engages people to think, solve problems and do the required things with lot of enthusiasm and motivation. It involves and immerses everybody together for a common purpose with empathy.

The most important benefit of Global Investors' Summit and *panchayat* has been that people have themselves become the brand ambassadors of Madhya Pradesh. The positivity is contagious and this is the hallmark of Shivraj Singh's quiet leadership that emanates from the heart and connects people to him emotionally and produces impressive results through the power of Global Investors' Summits and '*Panchayats*.'

Shivraj Singh to consolidate his vision, did one more exercise, he shared his thought process with the bureaucracy consisting of Senior IAS, IPS, IFS Officers and key departmental heads and professionals of repute at a workshop called '*Manthan*' at State's Naronha Academy of Administration.

Some of the Ministers of key economic departments were also invited.

All the departments were asked to bring with them their presentations and data with action plans to carry out reforms and development to make people happy. For doing this, each department had to proactively start a thought process for presenting and showcasing their ideas at 'Manthan' [churning of minds] for everybody present to have critical look and give their reactions, ideas and suggestions.

The feedback received from 'Manthan' that lasted for two days of 12 hours of deliberations each day, enabled TRIFAC to prepare an agenda for development and reforms for showcasing, presentation on Madhya Pradesh at the first global Investor's Summit at Indore on 26–27 October, 2007.

Picking up the right people for right positions to deliver results

Example 1

Rajnish Vaish, Vice Chairman of Narmada Valley Development [NVDA] of Madhya Pradesh Government was assigned a job to bring Narmada Waters into Kshipra river, under an inter linking of rivers project.

The Narmada water was to be lifted up by 406 meters over a difficult terrain of 47 kilometres. This project was dormant for more than a decade. The chief minister gave this challenge to NVDA in August, 2012. They got started in February 2013, and on 6th February, 2014, the Narmada water was pumped into Kshipra River. Both rivers got connected by just spending ₹432 crores within 14 months. Now the government plans to connect Narmada to Parvati, Kalisind and Gambhir rivers. Once connected in very near future, it would irrigate 16 lakh hectares of dry land and would also increase the water levels of Malwa belt, which has been fast depleting because of irrigation submersible pumps.

Just think about the prosperity it would bring to the people and perhaps Madhya Pradesh state will continue its agriculture GDP growth journey at a CAGR of over 20%$^{+}$ for next five years to be the number one agriculture State in India. Friends just watch out for the next agricultural revolution of India that is happening in Madhya Pradesh.

Example 2

The analysis of the existing scenario revealed that many of the schemes were lying incomplete due to lack of funds and other problems. The canal system was inefficient and water resources were not used effectively with the result that the water potential lacked coherence of various available technologies. To boost agricultural growth it was absolutely necessary to expand the irrigation facilities in Madhya Pradesh.

A vision and policy document was prepared by irrigation department by involving farmers, agriculture and Panchayat departments in creating this document and in 201 Radheshyam Julaniya IAS was appointed principal secretary of water resource department. He has a reputation of being a dynamic, upright and result oriented officer. He was backed up by the Chief Minister by assuring him of a stable tenure and non interference from political entities. The move paid off and the canal facilities that were less than 7.5 lakh hectares is 2010, today stands at more than 36.0 lakh hectares.

The Madhya Pradesh Government achieved the milestone by replacing lazy management of canal irrigation by proactive attitude and the factors responsible were fast tracking last mile projects; absolute support from the Chief Minister, boosting staff's motivation by recognition and incentives. The goal was to provide water to the last beneficiary at the end of canal by proper monitoring and follow up systems by constantly interacting with farmers on mobile phones [Innovative use of convergence of technologies].

Internal research and World Bank loan provided the necessary funds to execute the last mile projects – MNREGA [A job guarantee scheme] funds were used for de-slitting and cleaning of canals. Large numbers of water user associations were made active and were involved in irrigation management.

The support of the Chief Minister provided empowerment and a sense of security to irrigation officials to impose discipline and rule of law for canal management. No political interference was allowed and sometimes the Chief Minister directly intervened and that boosted the moral of the irrigation officials. The high performing irrigation staff were rewarded and recognised with various incentives. The direct involvement of the Chief Minister led to a greater coordination with agriculture, forest, revenue, *panchayat* departments and district collectors.

Peripheral issues were diligently solved and irrigation department remained focused on providing water to maximum numbers of farmers. Julaniya along with the senior officers of the department regularly visits the field operations to get the hands on information from the farmers. There are weekly video conferences that have brought in peer pressure. The senior officials randomly call up farmers on their mobiles. The IT has brought in a revolution in canal water management.

The feedback system allows irrigation schedules to be revised as per the demands of the situation and changing crop patterns and the water reaches the right place at the right time.

Lift irrigation from canals is efficiently monitored and charged for. Before the irrigation season, proactively all the canals and sub canals are cleaned properly following standard operating procedures.

Water supply managers are advised to operate all canals at full supply level as to allow the water to reach the tail end farmer's field and strict protocol is followed so that the tail end farmer is the first beneficiary of irrigated water supply. The water supply adheres to the canal rotation schedule that is previously announced.

This is governance, management and leadership at the same time that enabled Madhya Pradesh to raise its irrigation facility from 7.5 lakh hectares to 36 lakh hectares, in a record time of 4 years.

Example 3

Shivraj Singh has become an architect of tourism sector in Madhya Pradesh by placing Ashwani Lohani as the managing director of Madhya Pradesh Tourism Development Corporation [MPTDC]. Ashwani Lohani is not an IAS officer, he is from the Indian Railways and had come to Madhya Pradesh on deputation as Managing Director MPTDC thrice during last 10 years.

After turning around the Madhya Pradesh Tourism Development Corporation, his talents have been recognised by the Government of India that has now assigned him the job of turning around 'AIR INDIA' as its Managing Director.

The MPTDC, which was ailing and suffering heavy losses, was flagged by the previous state government for sale. Ashwani Lohani not only wiped out all its losses by 2011–2012 but made it a number one Tourism Development Corporation in the country.

The corporation implemented innovative projects like Bhopal Express, a train coach restaurant, a first of its kind in the world. Water tourism was a given a flip with cruises and a wild life safari. Many of its properties got 3-star and heritage hotel ratings.

The state bagged six national awards in 2015, all under the innovative leadership of Shivraj Singh Chauhan.

All these examples set the ball rolling for reforms and

development activities at departmental level keeping the big picture of making Madhya Pradesh a developed state in the next five years.

These are shining examples of 'Minimum government, maximum governance.'

7

SEEDS OF SMART CITY SOLUTIONS, GROWTH AND EMPLOYMENT – CITIES AS GROWTH ENGINES

In the smart city national contest whose results have been announced on 28th January 2016 by Government of India, three cities of Madhya Pradesh namely Jabalpur, Indore, and Bhopal figured in the top 20 rankings in the country. Madhya Pradesh was the only state that had maximum number of cities in the top 20 listing. This recognition mainly happened because of its participatory governance model.

Cities should have sustainability goals and should be prepared to adopt, adapt, improve, and innovate with convergence of technologies to provide services to its citizens and create a hassle free atmosphere for doing business and other related day to day activities. The city should be able to benchmark its performance through

E-Governance and convergence of technologies and smartness of its people. It should find ways of joining policies and working in a more cohesive and integrated manner across various domains like energy, mobility, ICT and water management, etc.

A smart city is also the one that harnesses the human capital and that has the citizens at the core, empowering with accountability and enabling them to co-create smart city solutions and attract investors to set up their businesses and acquire the desire to permanently settle down as a matter of choice in a particular city that matches their life style that offers them clean environment and services. Therefore now the focus of the Global Investors' Summits must be to attract the investors by offering the requisite environment.

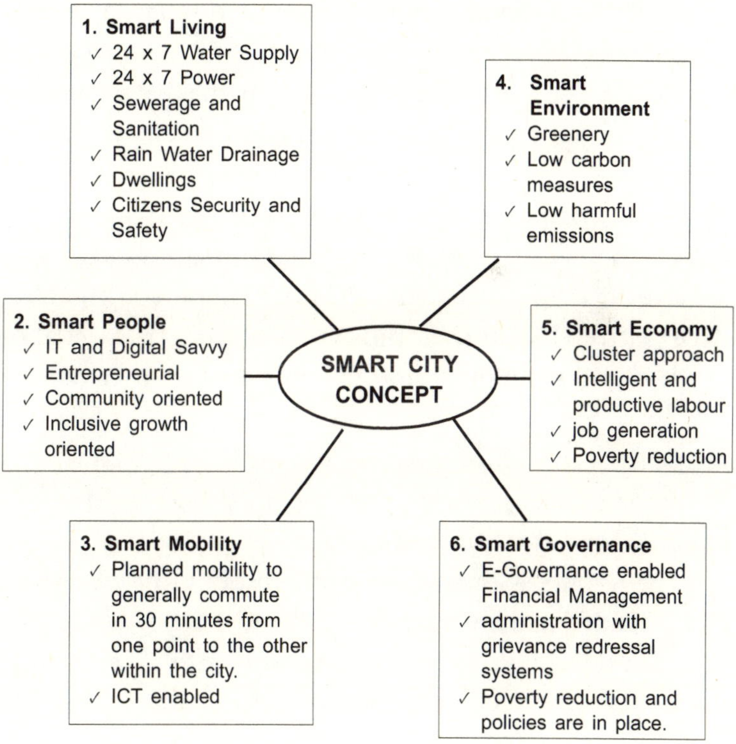

For many cities, becoming smarter means changing completely the way they work. This implies that a holistic view of city's strengths, weaknesses and opportunities have to be taken by analysing each one of the above for providing necessary impetus for the overall socio economic growth of the city.

The starting point could be to take a step back, ponder over issues with openness to arrive at a correct analysis of the situation to move forward to integrate all the parameters. Smart solutions will emerge out from the current dynamics of the city only by envisioning a future scenario with convergence of human technological and intellectual and financial capital.

Value added smart solutions have more acceptances since they bring in ease of operations and financial results. Awareness, cooperation, acceptance and peer pressure should be the part of the tool kit to make behavioural changes in the society to harness the full potential of smart solutions.

Collaborative working relationship between stakeholders is a must for success of smart solutions; to achieve this common shared vision is required. Therefore smart citizens should be fully involved in the correlation of ideas and solutions through living labs and technology and solutions should be used to increase social inclusion to combat poverty, citizens should be able to get sustainability, through greenery, sustainable mobility and eco-friendly environment at the lowest cost.

The strongest thread that runs through the DNA of a city is its drive to leverage the past and the present to play with novel technology and explore it to the hilt. This backed up by an advanced engineering degree and channelled work culture and right management to create the industrial power in clusters like Silicon Valley, Bengaluru, Mumbai, Pune, Chennai, Hyderabad and New Delhi.

As in nature, human beings tend to establish knowledge clusters that lead to wealth creation with least effort [doing more with less at low costs, see different and be different and law of critical few]. The start-ups are quick. They accelerate at great speed due to consistent practice of following 80/20 rule [20% of the things are responsible for 80% of the effect].

In clusters various kinds of expertise are available next door, saving valuable time.

To create an intelligence paradigm we need this infrastructure and attitude.

- ✓ Right kind of contributing knowledge institutes are a must.
- ✓ Various kinds of clusters are needed to provide different kinds of expertise.
- ✓ The city should have a holistic shared vision that should be fuelled by entrepreneurial culture.
- ✓ Citizens should have a sense of belonging to the city and the city as a whole should join together to achieve the holistic shared vision.

All the above, requires a set of visionary leaders who can bring about change by being champions to the cause, so that a revolutionary movement is initiated.

One such example is intelligence infrastructure is Silicon Valley that contains knowledge institutions.

- ✓ Stanford University
- ✓ Carnegie Mellon University West
- ✓ Silicon Valley University

- ✓ Santa Clara University
- ✓ San Jose University
- ✓ Singularity
- ✓ The Art Institute of California
- ✓ International Technological University
- ✓ Leavey School of Business
- ✓ Stanford Graduate School of Business
- ✓ Stanford University School of Engineering
- ✓ Stanford University School of Earth Sciences
- ✓ Stanford University School of Medicine
- ✓ Santa Clara University School of Law
- ✓ Institute for Business and Technology
- ✓ Cogswell Polytechnic College

Many secondary schools are funded jointly by State and Private Foundation funds.

Top Ten Universities that fuel Silicon Valley start-ups

- ✓ Stanford University
- ✓ Harvey Mudd College
- ✓ MIT
- ✓ Yale University
- ✓ Dartmouth College
- ✓ Princeton University
- ✓ Harvard University
- ✓ Brown University
- ✓ University of California Berkeley

Smart cities need 'Ease of doing business'

The Government of Madhya Pradesh [GoMP] has set a target to be at the top in the national rankings on ease of doing business.

In view of this, the GoMP has initiated several initiatives to improve the ease of doing business in the state. The department-wise specific initiatives are listed here.

Commerce, Industries **and** Employment Departments Empowered Single-window System

- ✓ Online filing and tracking of 'Intention to invest' on www.invest.mp.gov.in with dedicated relationship manager.
- ✓ Online filing of EM 1 and EM II with instant acknowledgement.
- ✓ Online allotment of industrial land.
- ✓ Online building permission.
- ✓ Online water connection in industrial areas.
- ✓ Online registration of partnership firms.
- ✓ Online payment of dues in industrial areas.

Fiscal Incentives

- ✓ All fiscal incentives given under Single-window system.
- ✓ No separate registration is required.
- ✓ Online submission at TRIFAC/AKVN offices.
- ✓ VAT and CST refund payment directly processed into organisation's account.
- ✓ Advance reimbursement with no pre-requisite for assessment.

Allotment of Land in Industrial Areas

- ✓ Online allotment of land in Industrial area through Single-window system.
- ✓ Land in Industrial area reserved for,
  - MSME–20%

- ▸ Warehousing–10%
- ▸ Residential and Commercial–25%
- ▸ Auxiliary–5%

✓ Land shall be allotted on First Come First Serve basis.

✓ Transfer of land on payment of 10% of land premium.

✓ Sublease is permissible.

✓ Lease hold rights can be assigned in favour of banks/ financial institutions.

Registration of Boiler

✓ Registration of boiler is done online through the Single-window System.

✓ The permission to transfer Boiler from other state is also given online.

✓ The permission for Boiler inspection is also given online.

✓ The certification for registration and maintenance of Boiler is given by a third party.

Layout Approval of Industrial Areas

✓ Layout approval of Industrial area is done by TRIFAC through the single-window system.

✓ No permission is required now for approval of layout of land in rural areas.

✓ Deemed diversion for Industrial purpose.

Department of labour

Voluntary Compliance Scheme

✓ Self-certification under various labour laws is available through Voluntary Compliance Scheme.

- ✓ One register in place of 61 registers under 13 Central labour laws for all industries and establishments.
- ✓ Two annual returns in place of 13 for all industries and establishments.
- ✓ The units are now exempted from multiple inspections. There is now a provision of joint inspection once in 5 years under various labour laws for all 16 Acts at one go with prior intimation.

Factory Act, 1948

- ✓ The number of documents required to obtain new licenses have been reduced from 16 to 6.
- ✓ For renewal of licenses, the number of documents has been reduced from 9 to 1.
- ✓ Prosecution under Factories Act is possible only on permission by the Labour Commissioner.
- ✓ Time limit for availing the service reduced to 30 days from 90 days.
- ✓ The validity period of factory license has been increased to 10 years,
- ✓ The Factory Act is covered under Public Service Guarantee.

Shops and Establishment Act [Amendment, 2014]

- ✓ Online registration facility.
- ✓ Covered under Public Service Guarantee Act.
- ✓ Inspection in shops and commercial establishments where less than 10 workers are employed is possible only on permission by the Labour Commissioner.
- ✓ In case of violation, there is a provision for compounding instead of legal prosecution.
- ✓ There is a provision for deemed approval in case the

registration is not granted in 30 days.

Micro Industries

- ✓ Micro industries are exempted from MP Industrial Establishment [Standing Order Act] and MP Labour Welfare Act.
- ✓ Inspection in Micro Industries is possible only on permission by the Labour Commissioner.
- ✓ Provision of deemed registration/license proposed in five labour laws, in case the application is addressed and completed in 30 days.
- ✓ Provision of compounding of offences has been introduced in seven labour laws.

Department of Commercial Tax

- ✓ *Registration without inspection.. The state has done away the provision of inspection before issuance of registration certificate.*
- ✓ *Self-assessment. Now under VAT all dealers have* been provided with the facility of self-assessment.
- ✓ *Online issuance of statutory forms. The state has provided for the facility* of online downloading all statutory forms [C, F, H, E1, E2 etc.] with no human intervention.
- ✓ *Payment of tax. The state has provided for the facility of payment of tax online.*
- ✓ *A single ID, There is now a single ID Tax identification Number [TIN] for VAT, CST, ET.*
- ✓ *Rapid Registration. Registration certificate is issued within one working day based on self-declaration supported* by affidavit and certification of two neighbouring dealers.

Online Facilities

- ✓ Application of new registration for VAT, CST and PT.
- ✓ Application for amendments in registration.
- ✓ Application for tax clearance certificate.
- ✓ Filing returns under all Acts administered by the department.
- ✓ Making payments.

Additional Facilities

- ✓ Facility to view Dealer Profile to view transactions performed through his account.
- ✓ Verification of TIN, Waybills and Statutory forms.
- ✓ Enrolment of Transporters and Transhipment Transporters.
- ✓ Android based Mobile Application for Dealers and Department Officials has been started.
- ✓ Push SMS/Pull SMS service has been started to provide regular updates.
- ✓ A fast track cell for providing investment facilitation assistance has been established.
- ✓ To facilitate inter-state trade, rates of central sales tax have been rationalised.
- ✓ Entry tax on inputs like cotton, iron and steel, components and spare parts of motor vehicle, manmade fibre etc. have been abolished.
- ✓ Model sale deed format is available for property registration on the web portal.
- ✓ Online Property registration.
- ✓ E-stamping facility is available in five pilot offices.

Energy Department

- ✓ All related permissions are covered under Public Service Guarantee Act.
- ✓ Authorisation is provided to chartered electrical engineer along with electrical inspector, for charging permissions [up to 650 V].
- ✓ Online sanctioning of new power connection is under development.
- ✓ Pollution Control Certificate is no longer a pre-requisite for obtaining electricity connection for industries.
- ✓ Necessary documents have been reduced from 14 to 2 for obtaining electricity connection.

New and Renewable Energy Department

- ✓ Online filing and monitoring of all applications and sanctions for project establishment.
- ✓ Online payment of all fees in the context of projects under renewable energy through RTGS.
- ✓ Provision for round the year sanction of application for establishment of solar energy/wind energy/and mini hydel projects on private land.
- ✓ Deemed environmental clearance for projects under wind energy/solar energy and/mini hydel projects.
- ✓ Nodal officers will be appointed to coordinate with matters related to energy department in the context of renewable energy projects.

Urban Development and Environment Department

- ✓ Online Consent will be provided under Water and Air Act.

- ✓ Online Authorisation will be provided under Hazardous Waste Rules.
- ✓ MPPCB notified industries are classified in red/ orange/green categories. No routine inspections required in green categories.
- ✓ Total of 567 green category industries are identified for approvals under simplified procedure.
- ✓ Extended period of consent to operate for 5, 10, 15 years for red/ orange/green categories respectively.
- ✓ Online approval of building plan through the single-window system.
- ✓ The MP State has mandated conducting of a single joint site inspection for colony development permission.
- ✓ Digitisation of land records for property tax is complete for 22 municipalities. Work is under progress for 41 municipalities.
- ✓ Fire NOC is provided as a service through the single-window system.

Department of Agriculture and Farmer Welfare

- ✓ Online registration for manufacturing of fertilisers and pesticides.
- ✓ Defined timeline for registration included in Public Service Guarantee Act with a limit of 45 days.
- ✓ Clause 31 and 32 under 'Mandi Act' are being amended *to exclude warehouses from the purview of 'Mandi Act.'*

Major Investment Destinations

Government of Madhya Pradesh has identified priority projects for soliciting investment in the state. A brief summary of the projects is provided in this table.

S. No.	Name of project	Location
1.	Special Economic Zone	Pithampur, Indore
2.	Industrial Park	Pithampur, Indore
3.	Gems and Jewellery SEZ	Indore
4.	Crystal IT Park	Indore
5.	Indus Mega Food Park	Khargone
6.	Plastic Park	Tamot, Bhopal
7.	Industrial Area Kiratpur	Bhopal
8.	Industrial Area Mohasa	Babai
9.	Industrial Area	Sitapur, Gwalior
10.	Logistic Park	Shivpuri Gwalior
11.	Vikram Udyogpuri	Ujjain
12.	Smart City	Pithampur, Indore

Madhya Pradesh Initiatives

Marketing cities based upon its strengths, weaknesses, potential and opportunities. Cities have to be trumpeted and marketed globally by the simultaneous use of these mindsets.

Think locally, act globally,
Think globally, act locally.

The cities should be named in a manner that it attracts investments, investors and talented people from around the world. The names should motivate them to do their wealth creation activities in a preferred location that meets all their requirements.

Tourism promotion is key to attract people to visit a town – to experience and observe its capabilities, competencies and its social settings and work culture.

For example Indore can be named as a 'Digital city,' Bhopal,– 'Knowledge Lake City,' Gwalior – 'International Yoga City,' Jabalpur as 'Make in India – Defence City.' Ujjain – 'Marriage City' to make use of the infrastructure developed for *Simhasth* Event 2016. Satna – 'Cement City.'

An official marketing website for each city has to be constructed.

Benchmarking with Other Smart Cities

Smart solution would start emerging once the city is benchmarked with other proven smart city.

For example in Madhya Pradesh 'cement city,' Satna should be benchmarked with Jamshedpur Steel City. Analysis of Jamshedpur city would set up guidelines to make Satna a smart city for leveraging its strengths and weaknesses and learning lessons from strengths, weaknesses and opportunities of Jamshedpur city.

Similarly when we compare Bhopal and Indore with Silicon Valley, it becomes very evident that the knowledge institutions [National Level Institutes at Bhopal] in these MP cities have practically made no contribution to the ethos, pathos and logistics of Bhopal and Indore. They have lived in their own world of isolation and bureaucratic power. Therefore to make any city smart, the knowledge institutions' responsibility and accountability for the city concerned must be made clear and transparent through close interaction with them.

Fortunately all the business houses, knowledge institutions and banks etc. have CSR commitments and each city must remind them of their social responsibility to the city in which they operate, their symbol at rotary traffic intersections just wouldn't do.

One of the major reasons of MP cities have not become smart is the total lack of responsibility and accountability towards the city by knowledge institutions.

They have so far failed to inculcate knowledge culture in the cities.

Now is the time to do this as process of expanding knowledge and culture that can be expedited by social media and ICT.

Creating Business models for wealth creation

- ✓ For example J P Nagar, Arif Nagar and Kenchi Chola near Union Carbide plant can be a good location for retrofitting initiative like the 'Dharavi' slum in Mumbai since the area has skills similar to that of Dharavi.
- ✓ On analysis it is found that 'Satna' can be an important nodal centre for tourism because of its proximity to heritage, religions and wildlife tourism. All can be packaged at one time. Satna has rail connectivity to all major towns of India, nearly 200 passenger trains pass through Satna every day.

✓ Tourism area distances from Satna

Maihar	35 km	Khajuraho	117 km
Tiger reserve			
Bandhavgarh	112 km	Chitrakoot	77 km
Panna Tiger Reserve	110 km	Bhedaghat	120 km

This new initiative can open up thousands of new jobs in the tourism sector.

- ✓ Seeking cooperation of public and private sector for voluntary funding from their CSR funds and actively involving them in the city's development and welfare.
- ✓ Seeking support of knowledge institutions for their intervention in wealth creation activities. With their help and support knowledge and innovation centres and parks can be built in a very short span of time.

Smart Services

- ✓ ICT enabled services for sewer and drainage, city waste and its recycling and energy production, water supply, intelligently connected city roads and their linkages to state highways and national highways have to be rightly envisaged.
- ✓ Land, its usage and development
    - ▸ Industry department in Madhya Pradesh has already identified land banks in different cities and areas for socio-economic development with allocation [sources] of funds.
    - ▸ The department has already holistically linked up Government of India's project Delhi–Mumbai Industrial corridor with State projects.
    - ▸ For example Bhopal is linked to DMIC via Indore.

The industries around Bhopal are linked to Indore with a planned development of Bhopal–Indore road corridor.

- ✓ Air connectivity – Expanding and improving air connectivity to Indore, Bhopal, Gwalior, Satna and Jabalpur is key to the development of smart cities in Madhya Pradesh.
- ✓ Few more ICDs needs to be added for augmenting the Madhya Pradesh economy.
- ✓ A citizen's movement is required to make cities digital savvy, which shall in turn make the city smart.
- ✓ A business model for Wi-Fi connectivity to smart cities is required.
    - ▸ One suggestion is to make Wi-Fi kiosk [like earlier telephone booths], which can also generate employment. It would be a win-win situation for the service provider and the customer.

  The kiosk entrepreneur in the medium term can provide online connectivity to many people who are not technology savvy with a small fee for rendering them online e-services.
- ✓ Schooling in Smart Cities
    - ▸ The seeds of future are sown at the initial schooling therefore it is imperative for the smart city schools to foster creativity, innovation, entrepreneurship through convergence of technologies along with the conventional approaches to teaching. New way of schooling must ensure Innovation, new skills for new jobs, digital interface and strategies for youth on the move. The schooling model at Polo Alto could be the benchmark for making radical

changes in schooling systems in smart cities.

We may use the following approach may be adopted for conceptualising a smart city.

- ✓ Maximum value additions at right places with the dictum of doing more with less resources i.e. holistic optimisation of all resources.
- ✓ Digital platform for relevant data collection and data mixing for right and smart solutions through convergence of technologies.
- ✓ Use law of critical few to get insights. Benchmark insights against successful business models elsewhere.
- ✓ Emphasise on initial schooling to make the next generation smart by restructuring the present schooling system for creativity, exploration entrepreneurship and innovation. Palo Alto in California, USA schools could be the role model.
- ✓ Follow 80/20 rule for speeding up outcomes in the shortest possible time.
- ✓ Involve and persuade all knowledge institutions in the vicinity of the city to participate in the socio-economic activity of that city through effective and concrete contributions.
- ✓ Keep the last mile citizens in the loop for inclusive growth.
- ✓ Intelligent and judicious use of the land bank of the cities.
- ✓ Keep a right blend of agriculture, manufacturing and service sectors in the city's economy.
- ✓ Create business models for making city smart by getting acceptance and participation of all stakeholders.
- ✓ Use social media and peer pressure for achieving

predetermined targets and goals.

- ✓ Identify city's strength, weaknesses and opportunities.
- ✓ Accelerate mobility within the city.
- ✓ Identify mechanisms and champions who can take the city forward.
- ✓ Give an appropriate name to city to identify its uniqueness.
- ✓ Find ways for people to become emotional about their city.
- ✓ Make people aware about their responsibility and accountability towards their city and use behavioural change techniques so that they follow the norms of the smart city. A guide line for appropriate behaviour to all citizens must be given.
- ✓ Create world class services for water, power, transport [mobility and roads] and also make the city eco-friendly by smart disposal system and implementation of strict emission standards.
- ✓ Make community learning as a part of Smart City's ethos.
- ✓ Citizen should physically and mentally feel and experience that they are living in a 'Smart City.'
- ✓ Smart city must apply Information and Communication Technology [ICT] to enhance its liveability, workability and sustainability of collecting, communicating and crunching data within and across departments and third parties.
- ✓ Smart city's sustainability is nurtured by city's entrepreneurial abilities to faster growth in multi domains such as education, health, infrastructure and environment etc with a view to enhance knowledge and wealth creation.

- ✓ The ICT enablers should be able to weave relationship with citizens of the Smart City with a continuously evolving business models. Analytics, cloud computing and crowd sourcing will be the important segments of evolving smart cities.
- ✓ Create a cell of Smart City Council at the urban development bodies with inclusion of Smart City champions to continuously work towards evolving the city as a smart city.

Remember that the Smart city is the economic centre of gravity and generates 70–80% of the State/Nation's GDP.

Innovative Project Suggestions

- ✓ Forming an innovative SPV
- ✓ Form SPV with GOI + State Government Funds and viability gap funding in PPP mode
- ✓ Semi Govt. Organisations [Money from CSR Commitments]
- ✓ Select PAN city project from existing ones of city development bodies, Industrial Estates and Housing Board etc.
- ✓ Industrial estates could be a productive self sustaining job generation business model. This would automatically become as a model for Quantum jump in GDP. Industry department is already working on such projects such as DMIC and other similar green field projects.

Citizen Engagement

- ✓ Use Facebook/Facebook groups/ Facebook pages.
- ✓ Advertisements on Facebook.

- ✓ Facebook videos, YouTube videos.
- ✓ Webinars.
- ✓ Instagram.
- ✓ Twitter.
- ✓ LinkedIn.
- ✓ Wordpress.
- ✓ Reddit.
- ✓ Google+ and other blog sites.
- ✓ Make leading news papers, Local and national TV channels partners.
- ✓ Involve stakeholders through their associations such as Chamber of Commerce.
- ✓ Use of FM radio.
- ✓ Conduct Workshops and Seminars.
- ✓ Make city USPs as a part of ongoing investors summits by the State Government. This would give specific cities a global exposure through a direct one to one interaction with the Chief Minister, his cabinet, colleagues and senior government officials.
- ✓ Cities should create their own websites highlighting their own projects and asking for all stakeholders suggestions.
- ✓ Based on the above strategies, make formats to record the insights/suggestions/feedback from all stakeholders and include the key findings in the proposal and also acknowledge this to the individual or stakeholder groups.
- ✓ For making behavioural change, please refer to a few e-books on this subject like *Alchemy of I, You and Us* and *Influencers* available at Amazon.in.

Pan-city Smart Solutions

Highlight the following in the business model..

- ✓ Shared vision with the stakeholders.
- ✓ How the shared vision benefits all the stakeholders [inclusiveness].
- ✓ Why, how and what this pan-city Smart solution road map is going to achieve in terms of making the city smart.
- ✓ Key components and SWOT analysis of successes and risk factors.[At least three].
- ✓ Same methodology should be adopted for area based development.

Follow the guidelines of GOI

- ✓ Implementation frame work.
- ✓ Collaborative process.
- ✓ Financing Plan.
- ✓ Benefits and impacts.

How to Make Cities Innovative

- ✓ Synergistic shared vision for the city involving all citizens and concerned stakeholders.
- ✓ See different and be different.
- ✓ Think Innovation and novelty.
- ✓ Doing more with least resources.
- ✓ Law of the critical few.
- ✓ Strategies for behavioural change.
- ✓ Highlighting benefits to the citizens with inclusiveness.
- ✓ How the business model empowers the citizens with accountability.
- ✓ How it helps to take the citizens to the next level of growth and prosperity.

- ✓ Pooling of all available financial, human social and intellectual capital needed for execution of selected projects.
- ✓ Convergence of technologies and ICT interventions.
    - ▸ Make people smart, to make smart systems run.
- ✓ Timelines to be determined by exercising Pareto's law [80/20 rule] – 20% of things create 80% of the effect.
- ✓ Keep in mind to envision Smart City with a soul [vibrancy by heart and values].

For example – Designing a business model for Bhopal for innovations, employment and growth

Strengths

- ✓ Bhopal is economically and socially environmental friendly city and is the capital of Madhya Pradesh – the second largest State in India.

Knowledge Capital

- ✓ It's educational intellectual pool more 400 schools, 70 arts, science and commerce colleges, more than 150^{+} engineering and MBA colleges [together], 26 Pharmacy Colleges, four government universities and three private universities.
- ✓ A new Buddhist University has come up at Sanchi [45 kilometres from Bhopal] in 2014.
- ✓ Bhopal houses national institutes of repute.
    - ▸ Indian Institute of Science Education and Research [IISER].

- Maulana Azad National Institute of Technology [MANIT].
- Indian Institute of Forest Management [IIFM].
- National School of Planning and Architecture [SPA].
- National Law Institute University [NLIU].
- National Institute of Technical Teacher's Training and Research [NITTTR].
- Institute of Hotel Management, Catering Technology and Applied Nutrition [ITTM].
- National Institute of Fashion Technology [NIFT].
- National Judicial Academy.
- Regional Office of NCERT.
- National Institute of Design.
- CSIR's advanced Material and Process Research Institute [AMPRI].
- Indian Institute of Soil Sciences.
- PSSCIVE [Main skill development and Vocational Education Centre of Government of India].
- National Institute of Design.

✓ It's industrial intellectual pool has public sector unit such as Bharat Heavy Electricals, Railway Coach manufacturing unit and ISRO Master Control facility, Major private players are P&G, Crompton and Greaves, Lupin, Vardhman textiles, Trident, SEL, Dawat foods, HEG, Eicher-Volvo, Larsen and Toubro, Mahindra and Mahindra and Netlink etc.

✓ All the Major Banks, Insurance companies, Petroleum and Oil companies and financial institutions have strong presence in Bhopal.

Industrial Capital

✓ The Commerce, Industry and Employment Department of MP Government has proactively identified both the undeveloped and developed land for Industrial estates and clusters and already has the land at various places in their possession. The details of land available are as given below.

LAND AVAILABLE FOR INVESTORS [Position as on 31.07.2014]

Developing AKVN Industrial Areas

Sr. No.	Name of AKVN	Name of Industrial Area	Project Cost [₹in crores]	Area in Hectare		Nearest Main Town and Distance [in km]
				Phase-I	Phase-II	
1.	Bhopal	Acharpura	72.50	140		Bhopal 18
2.		Bagroda	75.00	127		Bhopal 24
3.		Jambar Bagari, Vidisha	25.00	40		Bhopal 60 Vidisha 12
4.		Plastic Park Tamot Tehsil Goharganj	108.00	-	49	Obedullaganj 8, Bhopal 50
5.		Babai	80.00	–	200	Hoshangabad 20

LAND AVAILABLE FOR INVESTORS
[Position as on 31.07.2014]

Summary of Undeveloped AKVN Land

Sr. No.	Name of AKVN	Area in Hectares	Remarks
1.	Bhopal [7 places]	1009.50	I/A Mohasa-Babai [Hoshangabad], I/A Kiratpur Jilwani [Hoshangabad], I/A Jambar – Bagri [Vidisha], Tamot, Pipalnare-Bairagarh, Gram-Beelkhedi, Raisen, Rusia-Perakhedi [Vidisha]

EMC Badwai–Bhopal

1.	EMC Area	50 Acres
2.	Project Cost	₹46.16 Crores
3.	Implementation Period	2.25 Years
4.	Proposed Investments in the EMC	₹260 Crores
5.	Proposed Employment	Direct 3,000
6.	Target ESDM Vertical	Telecom and IT Hardware

The growth of these areas in next 5 years is likely estimated to more than double up the industrial production which is currently of about ₹25,000 crores [US$ 4 billion]. The break up is given below.

	Total turnover [₹in crores]	**Exports [₹in crores]**
Mandideep	13,500	4,667
BHEL and Govindpura	7,200	1,950
Pilookhedi	300	50
Others industries/ Railway Coach Factory	4,000	100
	25,000	6,767

At present the industrial sector is providing direct employment to 28,000 people. This may go up to 40,000–45,000 people in next five years.

In addition to the development of Industrial estates, Cluster and IT Parks several companies like Eicher-Volvo [Likely investment ₹3,000 crores, land allotted at Bagroda], ITC Agro Processing [Likely investment ₹500 crores, land between Bhopal–Sehore] and an NRI for 'Medical City' [Likely investment of ₹4,000 crores, in the health sector. Land is being identified between Bhopal–Sanchi].

If the above projects materialise, Bhopal's GDP growth may touch a CAGR of 12–13% for at least next 5–7 years.

The Industrial growth opportunities are available both in the present clusters and new green field projects.

✓ Five Industrial estates within 80 kilometre radius.

Ease of doing business

- ✓ Trade and Investment Facilitation Corporation is the nodal agency for a single-window clearance system and hand holding for new projects and investments.
- ✓ On line registration for VAT, CST, Professional Tax, Luxury Tax and Entertainment Tax.
- ✓ On line acknowledgement of EM Part 1 and Part 2.
- ✓ For land allotment, building permission, water connection and fiscal incentives, on line application facilities on www.mp.gov.in.
- ✓ On line filing in expression of interest.
- ✓ Only state in India to do VAT refund payment directly to investor accounts.
- ✓ In land container depot at Mandideep whose capacity is now being doubled.
- ✓ 24 x 7 power and adequate water supply systems.
- ✓ Policy frame work exists for BPO/BPM, Agro processing, renewable energy, Power generation projects, Warehousing, Tourism, Mining and Technical Education and Skill Development.
- ✓ Bhopal being the Capital of Madhya Pradesh has the extra advantage that all head offices of government agencies are located here; resulting in speedy implementation of decisions and action plan.
- ✓ DMIC [Delhi, Mumbai Industrial Corridor] is just 160 kilometres away.

Social Capital

The social and cultural intellectual pool contains

- ✓ Museum of Mankind.
- ✓ Bharat Bhavan [For cultural events, art gallery].

- ✓ Laser Show.
- ✓ Regional Science Centre and Planetarium.
- ✓ Ravindra Bhawan [For cultural programs].
- ✓ Indira Gandhi Rashtriya Manav Sanghralaya Museum.
- ✓ Villages around Bhopal are being developed as smart villages.

The Environmental Capital

- ✓ It's the greenest city in India [Cities having population of more than 15 lakh – Rediff Survey]
- ✓ It is presently ranked 27th least polluted city among 102 major cities of Asia.
- ✓ The population density ratio per square kilometre is 854, which is far less than metros like Mumbai. Delhi, Kolkata and Chennai [all metros have population density of over 20,000 per square kilometre].
- ✓ There are 16 water bodies around Bhopal. Bhopal people are emotionally attached to Upper Lake [Area 31 square kilometres]
- ✓ National park within the city limits and 3.5 kilometres of roads per square kilometre of area.

Heritage Capital

- ✓ Two UNESCO sites within 50 kilometre radius [Sanchi – A Buddhist site, Bhimbetka for rock painting which are prehistoric].
- ✓ Taj ul Masjid [the largest mosque in Asia] and other heritage buildings like Gohar Mahal, Sadar Manzil and Islam Nagar.

Health Capital

- ✓ AIIMS.

- ✓ Five Medical Colleges.
- ✓ BMHRC.
- ✓ Bansal Hospital.

Other Advantages

- ✓ Bhopal has a robust road infrastructure and has the best roads among all Madhya Pradesh cities. The average commuting time by motorised transport within the city is less than 30 minutes. Barring occasional congestions, the city traffic moves at a fast pace. Several cycle tracks have been laid and few more are planned.
- ✓ Bhopal has an international airport.
- ✓ Nearly 430 passenger train pass through Bhopal direct trains are available to all states of India excepting Assam, Himachal and North east.
- ✓ Various survey's and reports suggest that Bhopal is one of the top 20 growing cities of India and one of the top 100 fastest growing city in the world.
- ✓ Adequate water and 24 x 7 power supply.
    - ▸ Bhopal is a well planned young city and therefore it is much easier to take up physical infrastructure projects on a fast-track mode especially drainage and sewer systems and 24 x 7 water supply.
- ✓ It's an ideal place for green field projects.

Weaknesses

- ✓ There is little integrated effort by all the stakeholders to make it a great city.
- ✓ Slow pace of digitisation.
- ✓ Lack of self awareness and collective awareness for citizens to work towards the shared vision.

Suggested Socio-Economic business models for Bhopal's growth

The right kind of seeds is already available in Bhopal's DNA for it to become a Smart City at an accelerated pace.

How to make Bhopal a smart city?

It should have sustainability goals and should be prepared to adopt, improve, innovate and converge technologies to provide services to its citizen and create an hassle free atmosphere for doing business and other related day to day activities. The city should be able to benchmark its performance through E-Governance and Convergence of technologies and its people.

A smart city is also the one that harnesses is the human capital and that has the citizens at the core, empowering with accountability and enabling them to co-create smart city solutions.

Value added smart solutions have more acceptances since they bring in ease of operation and financial results.

Collaborative working relationship between stakeholders is a must for success of smart solutions; to achieve this common shared vision is required. Therefore smart citizens should be fully involved in the correlation of ideas and solutions through living labs and technology and solutions should be used to increase social inclusion to combat poverty. Bhopal citizens should be able to get sustainability, through greenery, sustainable mobility and eco friendly environment at the lowest cost.

Converting Bhopal's strengths and weaknesses into opportunities and facilitate job generation

- ✓ Eco- and heritage tourism.
- ✓ Medical tourism.
- ✓ Conference destination for industry/business meetings.
- ✓ Bhopal as a one point shopping place for power sector.
- ✓ Innovation and Convergence of Technologies through synergy and integrated efforts from knowledge institutions located at Bhopal.
- ✓ Substantial increase in industrial output fuelled by new industrial estate and clusters at Acharpura, Bagroda and IT Park and also through proposed Bhopal-Indore corridor that will have twin advantages of Bhopal and Indore cities and nearby area.
- ✓ Employment generation – the development of these clusters shall provide direct jobs to more than 15,000 people.
- ✓ Digitisation.
- ✓ Creating intelligence infrastructure with the help and cooperation of all stakeholders. Addition like Science Museum and innovation and incubation centers can quickly change the development scenario of Bhopal.
- ✓ Pollution levels can be minimised because the city will have a natural gas distribution for domestic use soon.

Bhopal's identity should reflect its strengths and opportunities. Therefore to mobilise Bhopal citizens to attract investment as also inspire talented people to make Bhopal as their home, Bhopal city should be depicted and marketed as **'Multi opportunities eco lake city' or 'Knowledge Lake City'**

Holistic Business models should be weaved on these ideas.

✓ Make Bhopal an electric goods hub. Bhopal with Bharat Heavy Electricals [BHEL], Crompton Greaves, Andritz Hydro India Pvt. Ltd. and GEI etc. as major power plant equipment manufacturers. Bhopal has more than 300 MSME electrical units that make electrical goods.

- World renowned companies like Siemens and ABB are already sourcing their power plant equipment from Bhopal. Bhopal units have competencies in making steam turbines, water turbines, wind turbines, transformers, and insulators and fabricated transmission towers.
- The total exports from electrical goods are already in the vicinity of US$500 million.
- The idea is to make an intelligent physical infrastructure to harness the potential of this sector.
- In addition Bhopal has a trained man power pool of more than 5,000 retired personnel, who are experienced and trained in manufacture of power equipment and are in the age group of 60–70 years. This human capital should be effectively utilised for making Bhopal a global power sector hub.

✓ Synergetic Institutional model for knowledge economy.

- Almost all kinds of knowledge institutions of National repute are present in Bhopal. Bhopal has to draw out a mechanism to use the potential of each one of them in a holistic manner and seek approval for cooperation from each of these institutes to collectively put Bhopal as a global knowledge city.

- ✓ Entrepreneurship innovation and incubation centre under an umbrella of SPV may be initiated with equity funding from various institutions from their CSR commitment fund. The State Government can participate by way of land equity.
- ✓ Bhopal has 16 water bodies and its fish production can be doubled within a short time by using smart technologies and processes. This has the potential of providing jobs to 7,000–8,000 additional people.
- ✓ The help on voluntary basis of technical colleges [around 100 in numbers] should be taken to train the citizen of Bhopal on digital awareness.
- ✓ The key features of 'Advantage Bhopal' should be ceaselessly propagated so that talented people set up their businesses at Bhopal.
- ✓ Create strategies and business model to make Bhopal as one of the best eco-cities in the world.
- ✓ Serious efforts should be made to improve Bhopal's air connectivity.
- ✓ An international stadium for cricket and other sporting events must be planned to make Bhopal as a favoured sports tourism destination.
- ✓ The setting up of Buddhist University is attracting Buddhist from all over the world to Sanchi and this would open new opportunities and links for tourism to Bhopal and its connectivity to Buddhists circuit tourism.
- ✓ Many business houses have shown interest in setting up their green field projects around Bhopal that would

lead to accelerated growth of Bhopal as a mother town.

✓ The slum areas of J P Nagar, Arif Nagar and Kenchi Chhola have expertise in garment stitching, recycling of goods and repairing of various goods and items. This is the most affected area of Union Carbide gas disaster. It may be prudent to allot some of the adjacent Union Carbide land for recycled goods market and for services like stitching, electrical repair/ recycling and plumbing etc. Reconstruct the slums in this area like Dharavi in Mumbai. These people have skills similar to the Dharavi [Mumbai] residents.

Bhopal is an ideal city to be developed as a Smart City since it has spaces for retrofitting [heritage sites], redevelopment [TT Nagar, Arera Colony and BHEL] and green field areas already allotted for Industrial use and IT park development around Bhopal. In addition 20 villages in the vicinity of Bhopal are being developed as smart villages. Since Bhopal has adequate water supply and 24 hrs uninterrupted power supply it has the potential to become the best smart city in India. The one pan city solution, which can quickly transform Bhopal, is to focus on waste management with people's active participation.

8

TRADE AND INVESTMENT FACILITATION CORPORATION [TRIFAC] – AS A GROWTH ENGINE

HOW TRIFAC OPERATES

Trade and Investment Facilitation Corporation Limited, popularly known as TRIFAC is a Government of Madhya Pradesh Undertaking, formed in the year 2004. TRIFAC has been designated as nodal agency for extending the customised package of incentives to Mega Projects [Investments of more than 25 crores] through Cabinet Committee on Investment Promotion headed by Hon'ble Chief Minister. Their portal allows investors to apply online for various services offered by Commerce Industry and Employment Department like Land Allotment, Land Transfer, Land Booking, Building Permission, Water Allocation etc.

Madhya Pradesh Trade and Investment Facilitation Corporation Limited

- Madhya Pradesh Trade and Investment Facilitation Corporation Limited [TRIFAC] formerly known as Madhya Pradesh Export Corporation Limited is a Company established under Companies Act 1956 and wholly owned by Government of Madhya Pradesh. [Certificate of Incorporation] Since 2004, TRIFAC is functioning as Single-window Facilitation Centre for Investment promotion in Madhya Pradesh.

Objectives

- To facilitate industry, investment and employment generation in Madhya Pradesh.
- To function as a secretariat for implementing the single-window system for project clearance, implementation and policy formulation.
- To provide effective pre-investment and post investment service by establishing co-ordination between different agencies and act as an interface between entrepreneurs and the Government.

  With active participation in the continuous development process of both agriculture and industry to create the right business environment in the State with guidance on policy and regulatory measures.

Single-window System

- This System allows investors to apply online for various services offered by Commerce Industry and Employment Department like Land Allotment, Land

Transfer, Land Booking, Building Permission, Water Allocation etc.

Activities undertaken by TRIFAC

- **Cabinet Committee on Investment Promotion. TRIFAC is an Empowered Single-window Secretariat for Mega Projects with investments of over** ₹25 crores [US$3 million] and also for Thrust Sector Projects of over ₹10 crores. For the projects in these categories TRIFAC pilots the proposal to the Cabinet Committee headed by the Chief Minister where a customised economic package is sanctioned, which may include fiscal concessions, tax exemption and all the facilitation concerned with industrial development committee that comprises of Industry Minister, Finance Minister, Commercial Tax Minister and Chief Secretary acts as its Secretary, and Principal Secretary [Commerce, Industry and Employment] is the Co-Secretary.
- Madhya Pradesh Investment Facilitation Act 2008. In order to see the speedy and time bound disposal of the applications of the investors for various clearances/consents/permissions/approvals, State Government has passed an act namely Madhya Pradesh Investment Facilitation Act 2008. Under this Act, three tier committees i.e. Cabinet Committee on Investment Promotion and District Level Committee have been formed to ensure the quick and timely disposal of the investor's applications at various levels. These Committees are also empowered to extend the facilitation to the investors as and when

it is needed. TRIFAC is responsible to act as member secretary for Apex and State Level Committee.

- Combined Application Form. Under the MP Investment Facilitation Act, 2008 preparation of a Combined Application Form has been envisaged. The process to have a combined application form has been initiated by the State Government for the use of entrepreneurs whose projects are to be submitted to the Apex Level or State Level or District Level Committee. When implemented, by applying with this single form, entrepreneurs would be able to get the necessary clearances in all the concerned departments as specified in the Facilitation Act.
- Investment Drive. In order to see the inflow of Investment in the State, Government of Madhya Pradesh has mandated TRIFAC to initiate the Investment Drive. In this process, TRIFAC has been organising the Investors' Meet and Industry Interactive Sessions, Road Shows in India and abroad to attract the investors in the State for making investments in various sectors. State has witnessed over whelming response shown by the investors from all corners of the Country and abroad. In the past years TRIFAC has successfully organised the Investors' Meets at Khajuraho, Indore, Jabalpur, Sagar and Gwalior, Industry Interactive Sessions at Bengaluru, Mumbai and New Delhi, Road Shows in US, UK, Australia, Japan, Germany, Netherland, Argentina, Belgium, China, Japan, South Korea and Italy, etc. Overseas Investors have also shown keen interest to choose Madhya Pradesh as preferred Investment Destination. The Global Investors'

Summit–V is scheduled to be held in October 2016 at Indore.

- MOU. In order to extend the best possible help and support and pro active facilitation to a potential investor, State Government or the investor himself may request each other to enter in to an memorandum of understanding [MOU] MOU is a tool by which both the agencies, i.e. State Government and the Investor show their expression of interest for achieving the investment plan. In an MOU, the State Government shows commitment to facilitate the project, the investor reveals its investment plans. TRIFAC is the nodal agency for executing the MOU process for the investment plans related with Industry sector. For all other sectors such as Energy, Tourism, Education, Mining etc., the respective departments are responsible for execution for MOU[memorandum of understanding] There is a prescribed fee for entering into MOU with the State Government.
- Delhi–Mumbai Industrial Corridor [DMIC]. DMIC is an ambitious Project of GOI, which is planned along the dedicated freight corridor being constructed from Delhi to Mumbai. DMIC would be passing through six States. In order to utilise the vast investment opportunities that would be created through DMIC, including Madhya Pradesh. Government of MP has declared TRIFAC as Nodal Agency to implement the project in the State. There are two High Power Bodies, i.e. Steering Committee and Empowered Committee to decide the matters related with DMIC Projects.

Which is the agency that takes care of DMIC project in MP?

Madhya Pradesh Trade and Investment Facilitation Corporation [MP TRIFAC] is the nodal agency for dealing day-to-day activities related with DMIC project.

Is TRIFAC fully empowered to take important decisions in connection with implementation of DMIC project in Madhya Pradesh?

For effective and smooth implementation of DMIC project in the State, State Government has constituted high powered committees. One is Steering Committee headed by honourable Chief Minister and other one is Empowered Committee headed by the Chief Secretary Government of Madhya Pradesh. These two committees are vested with the powers to take appropriate decisions for effective and successful implementation of the project in the State.

What are the areas which are to be developed as investment regions under DMIC project in Madhya Pradesh?

Initially following areas have been identified as investment regions to be developed under the DMIC project

- ✓ Pithampur–Dhar–Mhow investment regions.
- ✓ Shahjapur–Dewas industrial area.
- ✓ Ratlam–Nagda investment region.
- ✓ Neemuch–Nayagaon industrial area.

Who are the project management and project development consultants for DMIC project in Madhya Pradesh?

IL&FS Technologies Limited and Lea Associates South Asia Private Limited [LASA] are the Project Management

Consultant and Project Development Consultant respectively for DMIC project in Madhya Pradesh.

Has the government of Madhya Pradesh identified any project to begin with the DMIC project in the state?

The Government of Madhya Pradesh, in consultation with its Project Management Consultant and Project Development Consultant along with other concerned departments and agencies have identified the following projects as early bird projects for the DMIC project in the State. Early bird projects are

- ✓ Economic Corridor between Airport Indore and Growth Centre, Pithampur.
- ✓ Management of water supply and waste water disposal in Pithampur Industrial Area.
- ✓ Integrated Multimodal Logistic Hub near Indore.
- ✓ Knowledge city at Ujjain.

What is Industrial Investment Promotion Assistance [IIPA]?

- Industrial Investment Promotion Assistance [IIPA] is a fiscal incentive given by State Government to the industrial units. Under IIPA scheme, 50/75% [depending upon its eligibility] of the tax paid by the industry is reimbursed in the next financial year which excludes the input tax rebate and purchase tax.

Are all types of industries eligible to avail benefit under IIPA scheme?

- No, the products/industries included in the ban list of the IIPA scheme are not eligible to avail benefit under IIPA scheme.

Is there any limit of benefit in the IIPA scheme?

- Yes, industries can avail IIPA, subject to a maximum amount equivalent to the investment made by them, within the eligibility period.

Does entire amount of tax reimbursed under IIPA scheme?

- The 50/75% of tax amount, depending upon the eligibility of the Industrial unit is reimbursed, which excludes the input tax rebate and purchase tax.

Is there any pre-enrolment or registration required under IIPA scheme?

- Yes, industries are required to obtain registration from the department exclusively under IIPA scheme. TRIFAC is the nodal agency for issuing registration under the scheme.

What is the procedure to obtain registration?

- Industries desirous of obtaining registration under the IIPA scheme are required to submit application on prescribed format along with the necessary enclosures.

Is IIPA benefit given to new industries only?

- New industries as well as existing industries undertaking expansion, diversification and modernisation are eligible to avail benefit under IIPA scheme.

In which file format should I submit the required documents? You need to submit the documents in the following format.

✓ Photographs can be uploaded in JPEG or JPG format.
✓ Documents can be uploaded in PDF format only.

Do I need to pay any fee for registering project with TRIFAC?

✓ Yes you have to pay, the fee is based on industry type and investment.

INDUSTRY TYPE	INVESTMENT AMOUNT		FEES
	Manufacturing Type	Service Type	
Micro	₹25 lakh	Up to ₹10 Lakh	₹500
Small	₹25 lakh–5 crore	₹10 lakh–2 crore	₹2,000
Medium	₹5–10 crore	₹2–5 crore	₹5,000
Large	Up to ₹10 crore	N A	₹10,000

Is there any fee for applying under Mega Project scheme?

✓ Investors seeking customised package from State Government are required to pay application fee in the following manner.

S. No.	Proposed Fixed Investment in the Project	Application Fee
1.	₹25–50 crore	₹10,000
2.	₹50–100 crore	₹25,000
3.	₹100–500 crore	₹50,000
4.	₹500 crores and above	₹1,00,000

What Are the Main Activities of TRIFAC?

- ✓ Front office of State Government for investment promotion and advice Government on policy matters.
- ✓ Processing of applications for customised package of concessions, exemptions and facilitation to the mega projects through Cabinet Committee on Investment Promotion.
- ✓ Grants Industrial Investment Promotion Assistance [IIPA] to the industrial units.
- ✓ Undertakes MOUs [Memorandum of Understanding] with investors on behalf of the State Government.
- ✓ Follow up action and coordination between the Government departments and investors.
- ✓ Facilitation and Coordination for implementing DMIC project in MP.

What Is Cabinet Committee on Investment Promotion?

- ✓ Cabinet Committee on Investment Promotion is a high power committee under the chairmanship of honourable chief minister. This committee is fully empowered to sanction the customised package of concessions and exemptions to the mega projects.

What is customised package and mega project?

- ✓ Package of concessions and exemptions sought by any investor from State Government which suits his project. Mega Projects are the projects in, which investment in fixed assets is above ₹25 Crores – Food Processing, Biotechnology, Herbal based industries having investment of ₹10 Crores and above, shall also be considered as Mega Projects.

What is the procedure to obtain customised package?

✓ Investors interested to avail customised package, may contact TRIFAC, which is the secretariat for Cabinet Committee on Investment Promotion. There is a prescribed procedure to obtain customised package from Cabinet Committee on Investment Promotion. Application should be submitted on prescribed application form, i.e. General Project Information along with supporting enclosures and documents.

Is customised package sanctioned by Cabinet Committee on Investment Promotion is Empowered Committee mandatory and binding for the concerning departments?

✓ Yes, Cabinet Committee on Investment Promotion is vested with the powers of Cabinet Sub Committee of economic affairs. Hence the decision taken by the Cabinet Committee Empowered Committee is mandatory and binding to the all concerned departments.

Do I need to register on Single-window System Portal before applying for any Service?

✓ Yes, you need to fill Intention to Invest Form which when will be accepted will create your User Id and Password for the System. You will receive your User Id and Password via mail and SMS.

How do I register in Single-window System Portal?

✓ You are required to fill and submit the Intention to Invest in invest form. Once submitted the nodal officers will review and accept the form and User Id and password will be generated in the system which will be intimated to you via mail and SMS. You can then login with given credentials and apply for the services.

I want to apply for more than one project. Do I need to create separate login for each project?

- ✓ Yes, you are required to create separate login for each project.

Will I receive any notification or alert on successful processing of my application?

- ✓ Yes. On successful processing of any application you will be notified by SMS and E-Mail.

How can I modify already submitted application form?

- ✓ In case your submitted form is under process by any department you will not be allowed to submit the form again till the form is approved or rejected by the concerned department.

Is it mandatory to attach soft copies of required documents with online forms?

- ✓ Attaching correct and authentic scanned documents will expedite processing of forms by the concerned department. You can provide the documents in hard copy form to concerned department if you don't want to attach scanned documents online.

Which services are offered by Single-window System portal?

- ✓ Please visit Services Page to see the list of available services.

What are MOU's and their basic objectives?

✓ MOU is a sort of understanding between the investor and the State Government in which investor discloses about their plan for investment and State Government shows their commitment for best possible facilitation.

What is DMIC?

✓ Delhi–Mumbai Industrial Corridor project is popularly known as DMIC project. Indian Railways are constructing a dedicated freight corridor [DFC] between Dadri [Capital Area New Delhi] and Jawaharlal Nehru Port [Mumbai]. This DFC is passing through six states; one among them is Madhya Pradesh. Government of India, all along this DFC have planned to establish industrial region, which is known as DMIC project.

What are the areas, influenced under DMIC project in Madhya Pradesh?

✓ DMIC would be passing through the border of Gujarat and Madhya Pradesh in Malwa region. The districts which would be affected by this project are Ratlam, Dhar, Indore, Ujjain, Shajapur, Dewas, Neemuch, Jhabua, Mandsaur, and Rajgarh.

9

FISCAL INCENTIVES TO INDUSTRIES UNDER INDUSTRIAL PROMOTION POLICY 2014

1.	VAT and CST Refund	75% of Tax paid for 7 to 10 years
2.	Entry Tax Exemption	5 to 7 years
3.	Electricity Duty Exemption [15% of tariff]	5 to 10 years
4.	Customised Package for Mega Project	Cabinet Committee on Investment Promotion chaired by the Chief Minister is empowered to sanction packages on project to project basis.

5.	Mandi Tax Exemption for Food Processing Units	Up to 50% of Capital Investment on Plant and Machinery [P&M] for 5 years.
6.	Special Package for Textile Industry	
	Investment Subsidy	10% to MSME on Investment in P&M upto ₹10 million.
	Interest Subsidy to new units	2% to 5% for 5 years
	Interest Subsidy to new composite units	7% for 5 years
	VAT/CST Refund	For 8 years on the Capital Expenditure in P&M
	Capital Subsidy	25% for establishing Apparel Training Institute up to ₹2.5 million
7.	Capital Subsidy [only for Micro Small]	15% of Capital Investment [P&M] up to ₹1.5 million
8.	Interest Subsidy on Term Loan [only for MSME]	5% between ₹0.3 to 0.5 million for a period of 7 years

9.	Infrastructure Development Assistance to Industry	50% of the Expenditure made in Infrastructure Development up to ₹30 million
10.	Infrastructure Development Assistance to Developer	15% of the Expenditure made on Infrastructure Development up to ₹50 million

10

LAND ALLOTMENT IN AKVN INDUSTRIAL AREAS

Land Allotment Process

- ✓ Allotment in online on www.invest.mp.gov.in also on the respective AKVN websites.
- ✓ Allotment on first come first serve basis.

Land Allotment Conditions

- ✓ Land is on 30 years lease, renewable for further 30 years.
- ✓ Land can be mortgaged to avail loans from Banks/ Financial Institutions.
- ✓ Land is transferable if the unit is sold.
- ✓ Allottee has the privilege to sub lease the land to its vendor or other unit.

Land Cost

- ✓ Cost of land would be 1.6 times of the Collector guideline rate for the un-irrigated land in that area.

- ✓ Premium will be decided by giving rebate on the land cost.
- ✓ One time actual development cost is charged at the time of allotment.
- ✓ Annual Lease Rent is 2% of the Premium and is fixed for 30 years.
- ✓ Annual maintenance charges as per actual.

Land allotment to developers and investors in PPP projects

- ✓ Land in government possession with defined land use will be offered through open bid.
- ✓ Developer has the liberty to allot/sub lease the land/ shed, building etc., to the units on the rates and terms and conditions decided by them.
- ✓ Developer will be permitted to charge the lease rent and O&M [Operations and Maintenance] charges during concession period.
- ✓ Land will be leased to the allot tee for 30 years which is renewable for next 30 years and the allot tee can avail all the privileges as per the State Government Land and Shed Allotment Rules 2015.

Strengths of Madhya Pradesh

1. People focused inclusive growth based political approach.
2. 24 x 7 power supply.
3. Adequate water availability.
4. Good roads.
5. Accessible and friendly bureaucracy.
6. People are non parochial.

7. TRIFAC acts as a Single-window entity for investment and growth of state.
8. Ease of doing business through digitisation of Governance process. [Please refer to Chapter on Seeds of Smart Cities]
9. One of the leading agro based state with highest GSDP growth in agriculture in the Country.
10. Good track record of law and order and industrial peace.
11. More than 30 National Level Institutes including IIT, IIM and Maulana Azad National Institute of Technology.
12. Robust Industrial Ecosystem and Infrastructure.
13. Digitised land bank of more than 26,000 hectares exists for Industrial Investment.
14. More than 30% area is covered by forest.
15. Bhopal and its surroundings are one of the greenest developed areas in the country.
16. Good living conditions and minimal congestion as population to area ratio is far lower than most states.
17. State has logistic advantages being geographically centrally located with excellent road, rail, and internet connectivity.
18. Five inland container depots – Malanpur, Ratlam, Mandideep, Pithampur and Powarkheda to facilitate smooth logistic operations.
19. One of the largest DMIC [Delhi Mumbai Industrial Corridor area in India] influence area being developed as an industrial infrastructure.
20. Two international airports – Bhopal and Indore.
21. Modern hospitals and health care facilities exist on major towns like Indore, Bhopal, Gwalior, Jabalpur and Ujjain.

22. Man Power and Land Cost are one of the lowest in the country.
23. Never ending tourist destinations with three world heritage sites and large number of National Parks and Tiger Reserves.
24. Enthralling biodiversity.

About the Author

Pratap Verma – a multifaceted personality, began his career as a mechanical engineer in 1969 at Mumbai. Born in Raipur, he studied mechanical engineering from Maulana Azad National Institute of Technology, Bhopal, which explains his strong affiliation to Madhya Pradesh. During past 47 years, Pratap has worked for reputed Indian and global companies. He was Industrial Promotion Advisor to the Madhya Pradesh Trade and Investment Facilitation Corporation (TRIFAC) and Madhya Pradesh State Industrial Development Corporation (MPSIDC), during 2004–2009. He was a member of the pioneering team that initiated the State Global Investors Summit concept that fueled the all-round growth of Madhya Pradesh.

He has written *Madhya Pradesh Growth Story* with an objective to make people around the world know the 'why and how' of the phenomenal growth of Madhya Pradesh, so that governments, organisations and business leaders can channel people towards personal happiness and growth.

With a passion to build leadership awareness among youth, he has conducted many workshops on leadership building as Secretary, Federation of Madhya Pradesh Chamber of Commerce and Industry (FMPCCI). He has written three e-books: *The Alchemy of I, You, We and Us*; *The Power of Attitude and Beliefs* and *Life Changing Poems and Stories for You*. They reveal the power of attitude and beliefs through life-changing stories and poems. All three books are available on Amazon.in and Amazon.com.

Pratap lives in Bhopal and can be contacted at:

pratap.verma@gmail.com.

To know more about him, visit:

www.facebook.com/pratap.verma.146